SEASON *of* the ROSE

SEASON *of* *the* ROSE

A Journey of
Spiritual Awakening

Amy Flynn Boucher

MILL CITY PRESS

Mill City Press, Inc.
322 1st Avenue N, Suite 500
Minneapolis, MN 55401
612.455.2294
www.millcitypublishing.com

ISBN-13: 978-1-62652-211-4
LCCN: 2013910121

Printed in the United States of America

Cover photo by Stephen J. Boucher
Cover design by Stephen J. Boucher and Tricia Kelly

This book is written in honor of my Lord and Savior, Jesus Christ, and my spiritual mother, Mary, "Our Lady of Medjugorje."

It is often said that parents are the primary educators of their children. I could not agree more. This book is dedicated to my parents, Jeanne Gladu Flynn and Brian George Flynn Sr. (November 24, 1938-April 27, 2010). Thank you for planting the first seeds of faith in me from which my spiritual awakening was able to spring forth.

Jeanne and Brian Flynn on Apparition Hill, Medjugorje, 2002.

CONTENTS

Blossoming

The Harvest

ACKNOWLEDGMENTS

I have had no greater supporter than my dear husband, Stephen. He always has put aside his own interests and desires to support me and our family on our ever-evolving spiritual journey—from the early days of dating, when he willingly traveled across the world with me to explore this unknown place called Medjugorje, to staying home full time with our children while I worked outside the home. I thank him for the years of conversation, exploration, and discovery, as we set out not only to write and publish our own book but to truly live our lives in a new spiritual paradigm. God couldn't have given me a more perfect partner, and I am genuinely grateful for our eternal love and bond.

To my dear children, Madeline ("Maddy") and Maisie—thank you for your unconditional love and for your sacrifice of time with me over the years as I balanced family, work, and many hours of writing and revisions. This story is for *you*, to inspire you to also see the world through a spiritual lens and to put you on the road to spiritual prosperity! I love you both with all my heart.

To my mother-in-law and father-in-law, Elizabeth (Betty) and Eugene (Gene) Boucher—thank you for always being there to help nurture and care for the children while Steve and I attended writing conferences, met with editors and publishing contacts, and spent time in various ways on this book. Your selfless example of love is enduring.

To my two editors, Barbara and Marna—you each brought different perspectives and unique expertise to the revisions of the book at just the right times and stages. Thank you for your support and professionalism in making this book a reality.

Dear children! Also today, I call all of you to grow in God's love as a flower which feels the warm rays of spring. In this way, also you, little children, grow in God's love and carry it to all those who are far from God. Seek God's will and do good to those whom God has put on your way. And be light and joy. Thank you for having responded to my call.[1]

~Mary's Message of April 25, 2008~

INTRODUCTION

I thought I was normal. I'd had many life experiences, but nothing could have prepared me for what was to come. I was born and raised in the small town of Bethel, Maine. I had what many would categorize as an ideal childhood. I spent many memorable summers with my family and friends. We played in the woods by the streams, fishing for pollywogs and wading through the rocks. We hiked up rugged mountainsides to the powerful waterfalls, which became our own natural waterslides. In the winter we skated on the frozen lakes, skied, and made snow angels and deep, cavernous forts in the front yard. In the other seasons, we still enjoyed the peace and comfort of the great outdoors and the genuine rural lifestyle.

We were an average middle class family of seven, with Irish and French heritage. I was the youngest of five children. My mother stayed at home to raise us, and my father was an educator but had extended time off during the summers. My siblings and I spent a lot of time in his oversized garden across the street from a local chicken farm, but none of us did much to help him out. We mostly went to the garden to play and run around the open space, which dad proudly assessed as five football fields in length.

As children we fought, as expected, but also enjoyed the experience of a large, close family. My parents were firm but loving, kind to others, and great examples of how to treat and respect other people, particularly those who needed a little extra attention. I distinctly remember my father befriending a local man whose arms and hands were deformed. He was kind and respectful in the way he interacted with the man, always greeting him with a big smile and warm embrace. He treated him with dignity when others might have simply overlooked him. My father's regular, friendly encounters with this man at the local corner store are emblazoned in my mind.

Both of my parents took a particular interest in helping neighbors who had special needs. Each summer for many years, my father drove a family friend on a long trip out of state so that he could spend time with his extended family, while my mother offered counsel and friendship to a neighbor who sometimes needed simple advice on how to navigate through a difficult world.

One day during summer vacation, my mother and I stopped at an ice cream shop, where an obese woman and her child were standing in line. I commented on how large the woman was and asked why she would be eating ice cream. My mother responded by pointing out the loving embrace of the mother and daughter and asked, "Isn't it wonderful how much they love each other?" That simple but profound redirection epitomized the spirit of my parents' compassion and generosity. I witnessed this at various points throughout my life and carried these ideals with me into adulthood.

On Sundays the entire family attended church. I never remember missing Mass. I am sure that I did on an occasion when I was sick, but going to Mass was a staple in our family. In fact, my father would go to all lengths to ensure our attendance. When I was in my teens, I remember his taking me to the local hospital chapel to attend Mass because we had missed all of the other services. Rushing into the chapel was our last hope of catching a weekend Mass. If we didn't get to this service, we would not meet our Sunday obligation. Dad may not have been a deeply religious man, but he did have faith, and he and my mother made a commitment to raising us kids Catholic. Going to Mass on Sunday was an essential part of that commitment.

When we kids were younger, our family involvement with our local parish varied. Sometimes we were very active, attending church dinners and outings and supporting the parish in different ways. For a brief period, I was an altar server. I remember dressing up in the white robe and feeling very important. I also remember the priest being very patient with my sister and me as we made missteps while carrying out our duties. One of my favorite memories growing up was taking part in a living nativity scene on the town common. I was about eight years old and played the role of an angel.

At one point, I also distinctly remember my parents trying to institute family Bible reading time. We all sat around in the living room on the soft velvet couch, listening to my parents reading Scripture passages. I felt a bit uncomfortable about it, probably influenced by my siblings' protests. It lasted for only a brief period. It was a challenge to try to tame a group of animated kids and get them to sit and listen to the Bible, especially when they had not been accustomed to it previously. But I give my parents credit for emphasizing the importance of our faith and instilling a spiritual tone and religious direction for us. They succeeded in building a solid foundation of Christian values with which my siblings and I all eventually identified. In our search for independence, however, as growing children and evolving adolescents, we probably all strayed periodically from this foundation.

Being the youngest of five made me very competitive at an early age. I quickly learned that I had to go after what I wanted. When I started to compete in sports I realized that what I really wanted were the trophies and medals. My parents laughed when they talked about some of the contests that I entered at local carnivals. Whether a three-legged race or an obstacle course, somehow I would rise to the occasion. I entered just about anything that promised a trophy as a reward. And most of the time, I came home with prize in hand.

Just before I entered the seventh grade, my parents made the pivotal decision to move our family to another town in order to be closer to relatives. At the time, I thought this might be a good idea, but I did not fully comprehend the challenges of moving away from the friends I had grown up with. We settled in the city of Auburn, approximately one hour from Bethel. It was fairly traumatic to move, but I made new friends and settled into my new school. By the time I entered high school, I was involved in a variety of activities. I was the editor of the high school paper and a member of the student council. I always played three sports during the school year and still managed to hold down various part-time jobs.

After high school, I left Maine to study at Clark University in Worcester, Massachusetts. I initially thought that I would like to be a journalist. In fact, I had received a scholarship from the Maine Media Women's Association in support of that pursuit. Once I arrived, however, I honed in on social work and psychology, and the journalism career went by the wayside. I ran track and played intercollegiate field hockey. After two seasons, I decided that I was burned out from competitive sports and took up more leisurely activities with my college pals. We spent most of our time going to parties, experimenting with hair colors, and philosophizing about the world.

During my junior year, I studied abroad in Scotland at the University of Stirling. There, I continued to pursue an active interest in socializing. I was essentially an average American college student, enjoying my freedom and learning about the world.

After college, I left for Boston to take a job in social work. I worked with children, teens, and adults with a variety of challenges and varying life abilities. Working in and around the Boston area, I quickly became exposed to serious and significant social and economic issues. Most of my clients qualified for disability or state aid. They often lived in federally funded housing and required basic assistance such as food stamps. They were on state health insurance plans and typically held down part-time jobs to supplement their incomes. In addition to these challenges, most of them had also suffered from a variety of mental and physical disabilities. The job challenged me in many ways and forced me to develop a level of maturity beyond my years. I was in my early twenties, dealing with clients who, for example, tried to burn down apartment buildings or broke into police stations. Some clients were at risk of losing their children due to their overall limitations. I testified in court, worked with doctors and attorneys, and spent a lot of time in the community, ensuring that each client had the support needed to live independently. I was a pretty good social worker, but I had to make a decision about my future. I had to decide if I wanted to become a therapist by obtaining a master's degree in social work or go into administration in the social services field. I ultimately concluded that I could not afford to get a master's degree in social work. The post-graduate salary I could command would not be substantial enough to cover the debt I would incur. I did some research and sought advice from friends and acquaintances. Eventually, I decided to transfer my psychology background and human services skills to the corporate environment, and I secured a Master's degree in 1998 from Teachers College at Columbia University in New York City. I always joke with people that I paid a lot of money to get into corporate America.

Fortunately, my career change paid off, and I started working in the field of human resources right after graduation. Since my first assignment, I have held increasing levels of responsibility and have been readily promoted to different and more complex positions.

In 2002, I married my dear husband, Stephen Boucher. In 2004, we had our daughter Madeline. Our second daughter, Maisie, arrived in 2008. We live in an active and thriving town in Connecticut near my work and lead a fairly simple but full life together as a family.

Over the course of high school, college, and my young adult life, I spent a lot of time exploring myself, trying to determine who I wanted to become and what I really wanted to do. I tried to pin down the one thing that would make me feel fulfilled and satisfied. I took up different interests, like travel, photography, drawing, and poetry, all in search of finding my true self. Like many other girls, I went through difficult dating relationships and touch-and-go friendships. Along the way, I made bad decisions, hurt people, and acted irresponsibly. I have had my share of struggles, mistakes, embarrassments, and regrets. Although I am not the type of person to tell all, I can say that I have done many things in my past of which I am not proud, some having farther-reaching implications than others. At the same time, I also formed great friendships and learned a host of things about myself and about the world. In many ways, I think my journey into mature adulthood was not all that different from that of most others. In fact, I think I am representative of many American women of my age and socioeconomic level. Perhaps that average perception of my life is why the miraculous events that started to unfold for me on September 8, 2001, were so shocking.

This story is a personal account of the events that led me to one of the most stunning events occurring in contemporary civilization—the reported appearance of Mary, the mother of God, in the distant village of Medjugorje (pronounced Med-jew-gor-yay) in the province of Bosnia-Herzegovina (formerly known as Yugoslavia under the Communist regime) in Eastern Europe. The knowledge of and insight into these particular events have dramatically changed my life and have the potential to change the lives of others who decide to embark on the incredible journey of Medjugorje.

This story is a reflection of my personal experiences; some might consider it a private revelation. I have done my best to capture the facts surrounding events as they occurred over a period of ten years and to recreate situations to the best of my memory using documentation from my journal. In later years, I became more astute at cataloging different events and incorporating them into this story. This story is not intended to be a religious or theological view of the events. It is simply my attempt to share my view of very special spiritual circumstances that profoundly changed my life. Some of the names of people in this story have been changed for personal or other reasons.

PREPARING
THE SOIL

"Dear children! . . . Your heart is like ploughed soil and it is ready to receive the fruit which will grow into what is good. You, little children, are free to choose good or evil. Therefore, I call you to pray and fast. Plant joy and the fruit of joy will grow in your hearts for your good, and others will see it and receive it through your life . . . Thank you for having responded to my call."[1]

~Mary's Message of January 25, 2008~

One

Haunted House

When I was entering middle school, we moved from my childhood home in Bethel, Maine, to a house in the city of Auburn. My parents decided that moving from a small community to a larger city would provide us with additional opportunities that could not have been realized in the small town we lived in. We also would be closer to relatives, and that would be a plus. While our house in Bethel was on the market, my parents searched for a temporary residence in Auburn. They found a large, stately Victorian house that was centrally located—we were close to schools and had easy access to all of the amenities the city offered.

The house was fitting for our large family of seven. Although not all of my older siblings were living at home at the time we moved, everyone would come home for short stays or visits during the two years we lived there. The house was expansive, with three finished floors, as well as a base-ment. It was absolutely beautiful, with detailed molding throughout, tasteful French doors, and beautiful stained-glass windows that arched upwards at the center hallway landing. There were five bedrooms, several bathrooms, and essentially all the space a large family could want. Yet I detested it from the day we moved in. Even the fact that I finally had my own bedroom and private bathroom did not appeal to me. I instinctively felt uneasy about my surround-ings, but I could not explain why I felt so uncomfortable. What I did sense was a mysterious aura that permeated the house and put me in a continuous state of unease.

I understand now that the changes occurring at that time in my life were some of the source of my restlessness. My family was on the cusp of what would become two of the toughest years of our lives. We struggled financially and emotionally to make the transition from our long-time home in Bethel to our new rented residence in Auburn. Although the family really did want to make the move to Auburn, my father now had a long-distance commute to a teaching job that was less than desirable for him at the time.

Most of my emotional distress came from the fact that I had been uprooted from my home, leaving behind friends and all that I had really known about the world. I was also in the awkward early teen years, facing the nat-ural challenges of development while having the stress of starting over in a new city in a new school and making new friends. Now I was in a situation where I didn't even feel comfortable in my own home. I could not bear living in a house that had become a place to avoid instead of a place of respite or comfort.

4

After the move was completed, we learned that the previous owner was a local doctor who operated his practice out of the corner room on the first floor. The old medical equipment was still there and remained in place for the duration of our stay. Most of what had been left appeared antiquated. Some pieces were distinguishable, like the swinging magnifying lamp and the examination table, but others were more peculiar. Many of these large, bulky, gray medical fixtures were stacked against each other, creating barriers that made it difficult to walk through the room. Because of that, we only entered the room to use the sink. The room, although cluttered, somehow seemed vacant. The absence of color or light made it feel sterile and lifeless. I wondered what might have occurred in this room over the many years of servicing patients. I asked myself, *How many patients came through these doors? What ailments did they have? Did anyone ever die in this room? In this house?*

At one point during the time we were there, I learned that the doctor himself had actually died in the center room that had become the formal dining room. That knowledge contributed to my heightened anxiety when certain inexplicable events began to occur throughout the house and especially in my bedroom. We knew the doctor had died there, but I soon became adamant that someone else must have as well, possibly a patient or several patients.

The experiences that unfolded over the course of two years terrified me, and made me quite certain that the house was haunted. On the night of the first incident, I was in my room getting ready to go to sleep. I had taken a yellow nightshirt out of the dresser and placed it on the bed. I went into the adjoining bathroom to brush my teeth. When

I came out of the bathroom, my shirt was no longer where I placed it. I looked everywhere—under the covers, beneath the bed, in the crack between the wall and the bed, and in every other part of the room. My shirt was nowhere to be found. I was stunned and perplexed. How could my shirt simply disappear? I went to the dresser, retrieved another nightshirt—a green one—and put it on. I got into bed, tucking in my feet and legs securely. As I began to doze off, I still was completely confused over the missing shirt.

The next morning as I was awakening, I felt like I was wearing something bulky. As I opened my eyes and looked down at my chest, I was shocked at what I discovered—I was wearing two shirts! Not only was I wearing the green shirt that I had put on but also the yellow one that had suddenly disappeared. Moreover, the missing yellow shirt was *beneath* the green shirt. How was this possible? I had no recollection of waking, finding the lost shirt, and dressing myself like this. I would have had to take the green shirt off, put the yellow one on, and then put the green shirt back on. Even if I had been sleepwalking, which I had never before done, this seemed like an incredible feat. At that moment, I wished nothing more than to believe in the sleepwalking theory. Yet I knew that I had not dressed myself like this. The question was, who—or rather, what—had done it? I did not want to face the answer, but a deepening fear of the unknown grew within me.

On another occasion, I was getting ready for a school dance and was alone in the house. This was unusual, as I rarely stayed in the house by myself and certainly not at night. I was too frightened to be there alone. If my mother wasn't home after school, I would visit a friend's house. If

I absolutely had to be there before she got home, I would wait outside in the garage, clutching a butcher knife for protection, until she returned. On this night, however, I happened to find myself alone. My parents were both out at events, and my siblings were busy at work and with sports. I was already very nervous because it was rainy and storming. I was in the bathroom on the second floor, curling my hair, when all of a sudden, the electricity went out. There I stood frozen in place, literally paralyzed by fear. I decided that I had no choice but to somehow make my way down the stairs and out the front door. My heart raced— no, thumped—as the terror of walking down the dark staircase engulfed me. I didn't like the stairwell area. Each night when I retired to my bedroom, I made the dreaded trip up the long, winding staircase with my back pressed against the wall as I nervously peered up toward the third floor through the old, dark columns of the railing. I wasn't sure what I expected to see as I looked upwards; in fact, the fear was probably much more about what I *couldn't* see than what I could. Whatever the reason, the third floor and staircase were always a source of anxiety for me. So, there I was, alone in the house, frozen in fear, and trying to imagine how I could muster the courage to make my way down those stairs. I took in a long, deep breath and then slowly exhaled. I then suddenly darted out of the bathroom and headed for the staircase. While making my rapid descent, I tested light switches along the way, hoping that the electricity would be restored before I reached the landing, but when I got there, it was still dark. I momentarily stopped in order to ready myself for the final dash out the front door. In preparation, I glanced quickly into the living room, almost as if to ensure that there was no one—man or ghost—lurking in there, waiting for me. Instead, I was startled to discover a dim glow emanating from one of the lamps on an end table by the sofa. I knew that was impossible; the electricity was out. If I thought I'd been scared before, my fear was magnified a hundredfold at that moment. My legs shook as I raced toward the kitchen and exited through the door onto the porch. I was so unnerved that I didn't stop for shoes or a coat. I ran across the street as fast as I could in my stocking feet to my neighbors' house. They weren't home, but I waited under their covered porch until my friend arrived. By the time she got there, the lights were working again. Together, we went back into my house and quickly gathered my shoes and a few other things. I was still upset and shaken and was relieved to be leaving the house for the evening.

Most of my family members thought that my experiences were illusions or created in my own mind. They assumed that I was reacting to stress or that my imagination was getting the best of me. My sister Kelli, however, knew the odd events taking place in the house were not natural occurrences. She, too, believed that the house was haunted. Since her early teens, Kelli had experienced a multitude of supernatural experiences. She often had what she described as premonitions or heightened intuition about events or situations. These premonitions usually came to her through dreams or feelings. She would have a sense about a situation or person and usually some incident would follow. When she expressed to me that she too felt some sort of presence in the house, it validated what I already knew.

One night while I was out with friends at a high school football game, Kelli stayed at the house by herself.

When I returned home later that evening, she was visibly distressed. She told me that several strange things had happened that frightened her. It started when my uncle came to the house, looking for my father's college yearbook. He thought it was in the attic and asked Kelli if she would go up there with him so he could find it. Kelli was uneasy—she did not like the attic either—but she escorted him upstairs and waited while he looked. He eventually found the yearbook and left. Kelli was alone again and feeling unsettled about having gone into the attic. She didn't know why it bothered her so much; it was just one of those feelings. She went into her bedroom and began ironing some clothes. Not long after that, her alarm clock rang and startled her. She thought this was very strange, as she hadn't set it to go off at that time. She decided it was a fluke. A few minutes after that, Kelli heard a loud crash; it sounded as if it came from my bedroom. She hesitantly made her way across the hallway to my room and turned on the light. On the floor was a shattered mirror. She walked over to the wall where the mirror had been hanging and saw that the nail was still in the wall, fully intact and unaltered. She picked up the broken mirror and looked at the back side of it to determine if the wire used to suspend it had snapped—but the wire was completely attached and unbroken. How had the mirror crashed to the floor if both the nail and the wire were still firmly secured? She looked around and saw nothing else out of place. She became more frightened and went downstairs.

When I returned home, Kelli and I cautiously walked together up the stairs. As I entered my room I could see that everything was as it should be, except for the broken mirror. I examined it, too, and saw that Kelli had been right—

the nail and the wire were in place. We both concluded that there was no way for that mirror to have fallen; someone had to have taken it off the wall and dropped it to the floor. The problem was that there was no one else in the house who could have done this. Clearly, something—not some-one—had done this.

There were many other haunting-type experiences in the house. On one occasion my bed moved across the floor and back again. It was early in the morning, as the sun was beginning to rise—my eyes were shut but I felt the warmth of the morning sun on my face. I was still in a semi-sleeping state when suddenly I felt a gentle sweeping motion as my entire bed rolled across the floor. It swept gracefully, like the pendulum in a clock, to the left of the room and then back again, to the exact spot where it had been originally positioned. My eyes were still closed, and I wondered for a moment if I had been dreaming, but the sensation had been so distinct, so real. I opened my eyes to soft light spreading through the windows, wondering what had just happened.

All of these experiences were unique and particular to my teen years but they laid the foundation for my firm belief in the supernatural. I knew from that point on that one does not need to physically see something to know that it exists.

I was elated when we moved out of the house after living there for two years. We ended up in a smaller, three-bedroom house about one mile away. I felt comfortable there from the very first moment and never worried that anything strange might happen to me. Only once did I have any type of unique experience there, but it was one that, surprisingly, did not frighten me.

One night, not long after our arrival, I awoke from a sound sleep to see a light streaming through the window. In my sleepy state, I thought it might be coming from the moon but it was bright, and as I turned over, I noticed that the light was shining against the closet door. I was a bit disoriented but stared at the door for a few moments, and then I realized that within the light was a silhouette. My eyes were in focus now, and I could see what it was—the silhouette of the Virgin Mary. She appeared on the outside panel of the door as a profile, and I was only able to see her from the waist up. She appeared gentle and peaceful. I closed my eyes and squinted tightly, thinking that it must be a dream, that I could not really be seeing an image of the Virgin Mary.

When I opened my eyes, the silhouette had disappeared. I lay there for a moment, not knowing what exactly it was that I felt. This was a very different experience from the others I'd had. I wasn't scared, like the times in the other house. This time, I was just curious. I felt a sense of peace and comfort, and I smiled as I fell back to sleep. This experience became buried so deeply in my memory that I completely forgot about it for almost twenty years. It wasn't until later events were well under way that I realized the vision in my bedroom had been a sign of things to come.

Two

Mysterious Clock

*It was Saturday evening, September 8, 2001, and my boy-*friend, Steve, and I were anticipating an evening out with our friends. The plan was to meet another couple at a restaurant in the town center.

Steve and I lived on the same street, only a half mile from each other, but we were together most of the time at my apartment, where I now lived on my own. We had been out shopping that day and were running behind schedule, so Steve dropped me off at my apartment and then went back to his own to shower. We were pressed for time, so I quickly showered and dressed and then called him to find out when he would be back to pick me up. I was concerned that we'd be late in meeting our friends, but as I was telling Steve to hurry, I glanced at the clock in the living room—it showed the time as 7:25. I knew that time was inaccurate;

more than an hour had elapsed since Steve had dropped me off just before 7:00. I was puzzled. When I got off the phone, I took a closer look at the clock. It still showed 7:25. Perhaps it was broken or needed a new battery. I glanced down at the watch on my wrist and saw that the time was 8:25. I went into the bedroom to check another clock; it, too, read 8:25. I went back into the living room, thinking it odd that the living room clock was off by exactly one hour. Perhaps I hadn't adjusted it for daylight saving time, I reasoned, but no—that was months ago and I would have noticed it by now. Then I remembered that Steve and I had been watching television programs the previous evening, and the clock had been accurate at that time—we'd checked it for the timing of those programs. *If this worked last night, I thought, why would it not be working today?* Although there could have been a multitude of explanations for this, my instincts told me that something unusual was occurring. And as this thought entered my mind, a surge of disbelief rushed through my body. At that instant I was transported back almost twenty years to the rented childhood house that I had feared and dreaded. I started to breathe faster as memories of the past hauntings pulsed through my body. I knew for certain that something mysterious was happening again. I immediately determined that something had actually manipulated my clock and changed the time.

Without a doubt, the experiences that I had as a young girl shaped this immediate and extreme reaction. Most people would not have drawn the same conclusion as I did. But most people didn't live with hauntings. It was not such a stretch for me to believe that some unseen entity had impacted my environment. All at once, I was filled with a strong sense of conviction and resolve. This time, I was determined to deal with the situation head on. So I took a deep breath, set my jaw determinedly, and made a loud pronouncement, saying, "Okay, whoever changed my clock, I would really appreciate it if you would change it back. I just moved in to this apartment, and I really want to live in peace and be comfortable here. I don't want to be scared. I just want to live here without things in my environment being moved or altered. That scares me. Whoever you are, I hope that we can live together in harmony." As I finished speaking, I felt a sense of relief and was proud of myself for addressing this entity. *There!* I thought. *I am not going to be scared out of my own place by this thing. This time, I'll be brave and face it. This is not going to happen to me again. I am not going to be run out of my apartment by a ghost or anything else.*

At the time when the clock incident occurred, I had been in my apartment for roughly three months. From day one, however, certain things would happen that made me uneasy. Looking back, I realized that there could be rational explanations for most of the occurrences, but when put altogether they nonetheless created a level of discomfort within me—as well as a paranoia that led me to believe that something odd might be going on in my apartment.

On my first weekend in my new apartment, Steve had gone to a soccer tournament in New York. I wasn't very happy about staying alone the very first night in my new apartment, but I had no choice. My other local friends were busy, and my siblings all lived out of state. I had a difficult time sleeping that night because it was hot and humid. I hesitated to open the windows, though, because I lived alone on the first floor and was nervous about intruders.

I slept fitfully that night. The next morning when I went into the kitchen, I noticed that the digital clock was flashing. I wondered if there had been a power outage. Yet, at the same time, I suddenly became suspicious. I mentioned this to Steve when he returned. He said that it wasn't uncommon for older buildings like mine to have power outages—it often happened at his apartment. Although there was no real reason for me to believe that the power did *not* go off in the night, I thought it was odd that on the first night I slept there alone, something happened. Still, I chalked it up to the nervousness of being in a new place.

A couple of nights after that, I set the alarm for 6:00 a.m. and went to bed. The next morning, I didn't wake up until nearly 7:30—the alarm had not gone off at all. I picked up the clock and looked at the setting. The time was accurate, but when I checked the alarm feature, it looked as though it had not been set. I knew I'd set the alarm for 6:00, just as I did prior to going to bed every evening. I had been using that same clock for over two years and never had this problem. Steve suggested a malfunction occurred because the batteries were worn out. I did not accept his rationale because the time on the clock was still accurate, but I didn't argue with him. My anxious behavior was probably very normal for someone living by herself for the first time, but I also realized that my nerves being on edge were exacerbated by the memories and fear I carried with me from my childhood hauntings at the doctor's house.

On two different occasions, I had strong experiences in my apartment—very different from the more trivial ones. Although everything seemed to make me nervous, most incidents could be explained logically. The two strong experiences, on the other hand, could not. On two consecutive nights, I went to bed and fell into a sound sleep. Then, in the middle of the night, I suddenly awoke and sat up abruptly, gasping in fear. My entire body was shaking, and I could barely breathe. I looked around the room to see if anyone was there, but with the exception of my labored breathing, there was only silence. I knew that I had not had a nightmare, but I had literally been startled awake and could not understand why it happened. The exact same thing happened to me the following night; and again, I didn't know what had instigated my reaction. Steve and I discussed this and although he agreed it was strange, he attributed it again to uneasiness about the recent changes in my living situation. For me, however, the childhood hauntings, the odd occurrences in my apartment, and the instances of sleep disruption had already combined to create suspicion—and caution—within me. So when the time on the living room clock changed, I was primed to deal with the presence that I already believed existed in my apartment.

When Steve finally arrived to pick me up for our date with our friends, he pulled into the back parking lot and sat in his car, waiting for me to come out. I looked out the window, feeling a little irritated with him for not coming into the apartment. *Why is he sitting in his car?* I thought. *He always comes inside to get me.* I grabbed my coat and went to the car. When I got in, I told Steve what had happened with the clock and said that I was now convinced there was some sort of spirit in my new apartment. I told him about my pronouncement to the spirit, and I also realized that I was starting to get mad about it. "I'm mad because I don't want to live in a haunted place again," I told Steve. "I will move out if that's the case."

"I'm not convinced that anything unusual is occurring," Steve countered. "The clock probably just needs new batteries."

That night we enjoyed the company of our friends at dinner, and I didn't think about the clock incident again. The next morning when I awoke, I began to recall vague details of a dream, in which a faceless woman told me that Steve was trying to find out the size of my ring finger so he could buy me a ring. Somehow it was conveyed to me that his buying a ring was related to the end of December. As I sat in bed, I wondered if this message was of particular importance. The week before, Steve, his father, and I went to a psychic fair, where we visited a variety of psychics to gain a glimpse of our futures. There were people who read palms, conducted angel healings, read personal auras, and interpreted Tarot cards. We chose Tarot cards and hoped the woman who read them for us could provide insight into our present situations and reveal what might lie ahead. I attended these psychic fairs regularly with Steve and his father and found them to be fascinating. I was completely intrigued by the possibility that someone could predict what was coming next in my life. Certain information that the psychic shared would be very appealing to me, and I would focus on select insights. Essentially, I only paid attention to things that were really interesting to me. When the Tarot reader concluded by telling me to pay attention to my dreams, I was very interested. In fact, she said, "Pay attention to your dreams over the next couple of days. It is a full moon, and your intuition is high. You are going to get a message." To me, this was like hitting the jackpot. She told me something very specific, and I believed that I would indeed learn something in a dream that was relevant to my future. Over the week, I joked with others that I was supposed to get a message during the full moon. Well, the full moon came and went, and I never got my message. Although I made light of it, secretly I was very disappointed. I wanted to get the message. After all, I believed that it held the key to something special in my life. More than a week later, when I had that vague dream, and it had something to do with Steve and a ring, I wondered if that was the message that was intended for me. I was extremely interested in a future with Steve, so I hoped that this dream was conveying that he would soon deliver his marriage proposal to me. Still, nothing about the dream was very clear, and I was left speculating.

I got out of bed and sluggishly made my way into the living room, still tired from our late outing. I sat down on the chair and glanced across the room at the clock that had caused such a stir in me the night before. Until I saw the clock again, I had managed to forget about the events of the previous night. But when I looked at it, everything came surging back. To my utter amazement, however, I noticed the clock's time was now in alignment with the rest around the house. Last night, it had been one hour behind the other clocks, and now it was showing the proper time. Without hesitation, I smiled and said aloud, "Thank you!" Whatever had initially changed its time had obviously heard and honored my request. I was stunned. When Steve woke up, I excitedly told him that the clock had returned to the correct time. Although he hadn't seen it the previous night, he now acknowledged that something uncommon had occurred.

In a conversation later that day, he suggested that perhaps my spirit guide was trying to reach me. Based on his earlier experiences with psychics, he had come to believe that there are spirits that guide and protect us throughout our lives. He always referred to their being in the "white light." He reminded me that the psychic had said I was going to get a message, and he thought maybe this was the spirit guide's way of getting my attention. He said that maybe the guide had to do something spectacular in order for me to take notice, and that manipulating the clock was how it chose to do it. I liked that idea. Somehow, it provided reassurance. Although I was not convinced that it was a spirit guide, I did think that it could be an angel. I did believe that something good could be trying to reach me to protect or help me, which made me feel better, at least temporarily. I certainly preferred the idea of something trying to help and protect me rather than there being a ghost in my apartment. I also thought about my dream and began to think it was linked to the clock changing and the message about Steve, even though the message was still vague. I didn't mention the dream to Steve—it hadn't come at the time of the full moon, so I sensed that this was something *different* from what the psychic predicted.

It was Sunday when we had that conversation and on Monday morning, I woke up at around 6:00 and realized that I was actually alone in my apartment for the first time since the clocked changed back. I felt a very mild nervousness but then managed to fall back asleep. I had another dream, but it was unlike any other I had ever experienced. It was as if I was participating in it rather than viewing it as a spectator. Perhaps I was in an alternate state of consciousness, one that was different from the dream state. Everything was sharp and clear. In this dreamlike realm, I felt myself sit upright in my bed, and as I sat up, I noticed a very large piece of white paper taped to my bedroom door. It had scribbled words on it and I strained to read them. The writing was in black marker and seemed to be the handwriting of a child. It was messy, as if whoever wrote it had a hard time with it. The first sentence read "Thank you for thinking nice thoughts of me." The next sentence was illegible. It appeared that something had been written but was then crossed out. Then there was a long paragraph that also was crossed out so that I could not actually read the words. The content of the illegible paragraph, however, was conveyed to me in thought form. It had something to do with me and Steve and marriage. I specifically remember the words "by the end of December." That was the only specific information that I received. Yet again, it was almost as if I was given the knowledge without actually reading it. Other than that, I very clearly received a reassuring message about our relationship. I was told that Steve and I had a bond and that we had a love that was not limited to, and was even greater than, the love that we had for each other here on this earth—a love that transcended the boundaries of what we knew.

As I finished reading the paragraph and while still in my dream, I looked to the doorway, and there was Steve with a beautiful smile on his face. All around him was a white, glowing aura—a halo of light—that filled me with love in its purest sense. It was unlike anything I have ever experienced. I rose from my bed to meet him, and we embraced. Then, in my left ear, I heard the sound of children laughing and birds chirping. I felt pure love when I embraced Steve, and as I heard the children and the birds, I had a sense of pure happiness and joy. When I heard the young voices, it was as if I was being pulled toward them. I did not see them, but knew they were there. Suddenly, I was being taken somewhere, as though on a walk but not walking. I was floating, hovering above the street, and moving forward. Someone was propelling me along, guiding me. We made our way up a street to a schoolyard. Both the street and school looked familiar. It looked like the local elementary school not far from my neighborhood. I knew I was being shown this for a purpose, yet it wasn't made clear. Then, looking across the street, I saw a woman walking along the sidewalk. She was possibly in her late thirties or early forties and had reddish-brown hair that was slightly shorter than shoulder length. She looked very tired, worn and defeated. She was wandering in a confused state and appeared to be searching for something. When I looked across the street at her, she turned and looked at me directly. Without taking her gaze off of me, she reached down toward the sidewalk and brushed her finger against the curb. I noticed her hand was bare—she wore no rings—and as she scraped her wedding finger against the cement, it started to bleed. Then she looked right into my eyes, and her penetrating look sent chills through me. I sensed something ominous and was left with a deep sense of concern. It was as if I was getting a warning of some sort, but I could not discern the meaning. Immediately after seeing the woman with her bleeding finger, I was back in my bed, as if I had never left. The foreboding feeling was gone, and I was filled with an overwhelming sense of peace and beauty, the same as I'd felt throughout most of the dream.

I spent all day thinking about how amazing the experience had been. It touched me so deeply. I spoke to Steve about it, and he, too, marveled at the vividness that I conveyed—although I only told him about the message of our eternal bond and not that I was hoping that it had something to do with a marriage proposal. He was impressed by the fact that I'd had such direct contact with what he referred to as a spirit guide. Although neither of us was exactly clear on what had happened or what it meant, we both agreed that there had been a specific message contained in the dream, and the experience was quite remarkable.

On the following morning, Tuesday, September 11, I awoke to the exact same sounds as in my dream of the previous morning—that of children laughing and playing and birds chirping. The sounds lasted but an instant, yet I recognized that they were exactly the same. It was as if a soundtrack was being replayed for me. There was virtually no detectable difference.

Although I woke up that morning with positive feelings from the dream, I was beginning to feel overwhelmed and uneasy. The brave new me who dealt with the supernatural head-on was starting to get nervous and scared. I finally realized that I was actually communicating with something not of this world. I wondered who it could be and what, if anything, I was supposed to do now. I stayed in bed, trying to understand what it all meant. I started to get more anxious, particularly because these disturbances weren't exactly something that I could easily share with others—Steve was the only person in my life who would believe me. Even as my fears took hold, I remembered that I was due to join a conference call for work at 8:00 a.m. I got up and regained my composure. The call started promptly at 8:00, and I was sure no one could detect anything unusual in my voice. Approximately forty-five minutes into the call, someone interrupted the meeting to inform us that a plane had flown into one of the twin towers of the World Trade Center in New York City. We immediately suspended the meeting, and I ran to turn on the television. I watched in disbelief as the building burned. Within roughly fifteen minutes, I saw the second plane slam into the other tower. Shortly thereafter, the news reported that a plane had slammed into the Pentagon. Then, another plane was reported as having crashed in a field in Pennsylvania. It was like a horror movie, and I sat watching in complete disbelief. Like most Americans, I had never felt such terror or seen such destruction unfold before my eyes. I was overcome by grief and despair at the terrorist attacks against the United States.

These world-altering events occurred only three days after the clock initially changed and on the very day of my second dream. I was already emotionally weighed down by my personal circumstances. I was grappling with some sort of supernatural event, struggling to understand what it was and what it meant. I felt completely ungrounded. September 11 and the ensuing days, weeks, and months were draining on everyone, and they certainly added more stress to an already difficult personal situation for me.

Three

My Spiritual Awakening

The next week proved to be very exhausting. The overwhelming emotions associated with the 9/11 attacks, coupled with the inexplicable events that were occurring in my own life created a high level of anxiety for me. Steve and I went to dinner one night, and I broke down in tears. I wanted everything in my life to return to the way it was before the clock incident and the dream sequences. I felt so out of control. "How do you control spirits from coming into your life?" I asked. "How can I make any sense out of this? Why now? Why me?"

Steve was very understanding. He talked to me and explained that I could control the things that were going on around me. He asked, "Don't you think that whoever has contacted you can see how much this is upsetting you?" He was right. Surely this entity could see my reaction and distress. That night I made a firm decision that I would tele-pathically communicate with this entity to let it know that I was scared by its imposition.

For a couple of nights thereafter, I closed my eyes and formulated various messages directed at this unknown presence. I imagined that my messages were released out into the universe and were understood by the intended re-cipient, whoever it was. I also adopted a negotiating stance. At one point, I told the ghost, spirit, or whatever it was that I was willing to receive messages through dreams as long as it did not disrupt or alter my apartment or my environment. I was desperately trying to exert some influence over a situ-ation that wasn't associated with any reality that I knew. As far as I was concerned, nothing I tried seemed too far-fetched or ridiculous.

I had to do something because I was exhausted from lying awake each night, terrified, anticipating that some-thing supernatural would happen. I was constantly look-ing over my shoulder, not just at night but any time I was in my apartment. I was afraid to be alone; I was afraid of absolutely everything. One night I was sitting at the table, writing some notes. What was left of the bottle of wine we'd had with dinner was in front of me. Steve was sitting on the couch watching TV. Suddenly, the cork popped right out of the bottle. I jumped up, my eyes wide with fear. I quickly moved away from the table and positioned myself on the couch next to Steve, seeking comfort and protection. I'd developed a hypothesis that close physical proximity to someone else would prevent or inhibit this force from inter-acting with me. I also felt that this haunting was contained to my apartment, so if I could always have someone with me while I was in my apartment, then everything would be fine. Shortly after this incident, however, I had the startling realization that what was happening to me could occur anywhere, at any time.

I soon decided to go stay at Steve's apartment rather than chance any more disturbing incidents. I refused to go into my apartment alone, and Steve was wonderfully supportive. One day during my lunch break at work, we returned to my apartment, and I quickly gathered my clothes and other essentials. Steve exited through the back door, and I left through the front, almost sprinting to my car. I could barely wait to get in and close the door so I could feel safe. I had been so frightened, but now that I was safely separated from the disturbing forces in my apartment, I felt a great sense of relief and could enjoy staying at Steve's that night. I turned on the radio and drove down the street, heading back to work. When I stopped at the corner, I looked left to check for traffic, and as I turned my head, my radio suddenly went silent. I looked down at the radio and noticed that although the music had stopped playing mid-song, the digital display still showed the number of the station. I stared at the display, waiting for the music to return, but it did not. I twisted the dial to a different radio station and then immediately changed it back to the original station. The same song was playing, as if no interruption had occurred.

My heart sank. "Okay," I said to myself, "I get the picture." It was then that I realized that this was not about my apartment; it was about *me*. I continued to drive to work, and when almost there, was suddenly overcome by a strange, jolt-like force. It startled me so much that I had to pull off to the side of the road. I felt my body jerk slightly and my stomach drop, almost as it does when speeding downhill on a roller coaster. It reminded me of the way that movies typically portray the experience people have when a ghost or spirit passes through them; it was truly like that. I had never experienced anything like it before. When I calmed down, I got back on the road and returned to my office, but I was so preoccupied by the recent intrusions that I found it hard to concentrate. I walked down to the lake near the office and stared out over the water, longing to feel grounded and connected to nature—to reality. Yet all I felt was confusion, detachment, and fear.

By Sunday, I was a nervous wreck. I had not slept all week and could barely eat. Steve and I went to a wine festival that day with his family. The sun was brilliant, and it was an absolutely perfect autumn day. Even though there was a great band playing, there was a somber tone to their music and a melancholy mood due to the 9/11 terrorist attacks that had occurred during the previous week. The band played a lot of songs by musical legends from the '60s and '70s such as Bob Dylan; Peter, Paul & Mary; and The Beatles, to name a few. I thought of the era when these songs were first heard, and I still felt the trauma reverberating from the 9/11 attacks, and this caused me to contemplate what the mood must have been like during the Vietnam War, when people wanted desperately to understand the madness and the loss. I became very emotional as I listened, and several times I caught my breath as my eyes welled with tears. Then, they played the song that sent chills through my body: "Let It Be" by the Beatles. As it began, my entire being soaked up the sound in an intimate and personal way. It seemed that the lyrics spoke to me directly, as though they were meant for me and only me. The words called out: "When I find my-self in times of trouble, Mother Mary comes to me, speaking words of wisdom, let it be. And in my hour of darkness she is standing right in front of me, speaking words of wisdom, let it be." There was something comforting about those words and something strangely familiar that hit right at my core. I sang the lyrics over and over in my head, picturing the Virgin Mary.

When the festivities of the day concluded, Steve's family suggested we drive to a nearby lake to relax for a while longer. When we arrived, I started to unravel emotionally. I felt like I was on the brink of a nervous break-down and could barely keep from crying. I walked down to the water and sat on a rock. Steve's nephew was playing down there, and as I watched him play with such simplic-ity and innocence, it made my fragile emotional state even more raw. Steve eventually walked down to the water to see how I was doing. When he gave me a hug, I broke out in tears. I told him that I didn't know what to do; that I felt like I was crazy. He comforted me and reassured me that the whole experience was heightened because I was sleep-deprived. He knew that I had not slept much over the past week and said that I needed to break the pattern. "We'll stop at the pharmacy to get sleeping pills for tonight," he said.

I knew that he was right, and I resolved to gain con-trol over the worsening situation. Steve also suggested that I take the next day off from work and call a therapist, as well as call the medium/psychic that had recently given me a reading. I agreed to do all of that on one condition—that I did not have to sleep at my apartment. He agreed, of course.

As we started to leave, some of Steve's family asked what was wrong. Everyone knew about a few incidents, and I think most of them were not sure what to make of the situation. One of Steve's brothers tried to comfort me, telling me about an experience he once had, where he felt that there were negative spirits or influences in his apartment. He said that they went away once he dealt with them head-on. He didn't get into the details of how he did this, but it made me feel a little better to know that someone was relating to me and imagining that I might be able to influence the situation. All of the support was very much appreciated, but I still worried that Steve's family thought I was unstable and a little bit odd. Regardless of other people's perceptions, though, it still was terrifying to know that something was happening to me that had no basis in reality, and there was no way for me to understand the events logically.

That night I slept at Steve's apartment. I took a sleeping pill before going to bed and managed to get a full night's sleep for the first time in over a week. I didn't go to work that day and tried to make the two appointments Steve previously suggested. I called a therapist through our employee assistance program at work and also tried to contact the Tarot card reader with whom I had previously consulted. I secured an appointment with the therapist for that Wednesday and exchanged several voicemails with the psychic but was unable to reach her that day.

That night, I slept at Steve's apartment again. This time I did not take a sleeping pill but did get another good night's sleep. I awoke the next morning with the following words in my head: *Medjugorje, spiritual awakening.* I woke Steve and asked, "What is Medjugorje?" He asked me to repeat the word. I told him that I had woken up with these words in my head and that I did not know what Medjugorje was or how to spell it but that for some reason, I thought that it had something to do with people going on pilgrimages to seek out deeper spiritual meaning in their lives. We talked about it for a few minutes and agreed that we needed to find out more. Steve said he would research it on the Internet for me when he went to work. We also talked about the manner in which these words came to me—they were simply *there* when I woke up. It was as if someone had spoken them to me, but there was no voice, just the thought. The words came to me with a gentle purity, like the stillness of the night.

Shortly after I arrived at work, Steve called and informed me that he found a number of books in an online bookstore relating to Medjugorje. "Do you know what this is?" he asked excitedly.

"No," I said. "What is it?"

"I'll e-mail you the link and you can see for yourself."

When I received it, I immediately clicked on the link. As the web page opened, I saw that there were several books listed, and as I scanned down the page, I saw a picture of the Virgin Mary on the cover of one of the books. Amazed, I asked, "What is going on? What is this?"

Steve gave a quick explanation as I scanned the material before me. I soon learned that Medjugorje is a place in the former Communist territory of Yugoslavia, where the Virgin Mary reportedly appeared to six children. I was stunned. I asked Steve, "Why am *I* getting messages that have to do with the Virgin Mary?" Neither of us knew, but we were determined to pursue this. Steve started to provide more detail of what he had already read. He suggested that

I read one of the books listed on the site, but I was not sure which one to select. Then I saw a book with the title including *The Children of Medjugorje*. Steve reminded me of my dream, when I'd heard children laughing and playing, and suggested that was the particular book I should read. Then I scanned farther down the page and began reading the synopsis of another book. This one was written by a Protestant journalist and was touted as possibly the most compelling account of the Medjugorje events thus far. Despite my heightened interest in learning more, I simply could not decide which book to read first. What was holding me back? I was in search of the answers, but I think I was also afraid of what those answers would be and in what unknown direction they would lead me.

That same evening, I managed to get an appointment with the psychic, Laura, whom I had been seeing over the last year. Considering the urgency of my need, she agreed to see me at her home that evening. I made the forty-five-minute drive to see her, hoping to get a consultation with her—not a Tarot reading—on how to deal with some of the puzzling things that were happening to me. Given her work with the supernatural, I thought she might have some suggestions for handling matters not of this world. When I arrived at her house, she was very welcoming. She led me to what appeared to be her bedroom. She pulled out the Tarot cards, and my heart leapt into my throat. I tried to explain to her that I was really seeking her guidance on an urgent matter, but I did not express myself clearly, so she proceeded with a reading. I was wrought with anxiety as her hands massaged the cards, and she intently reflected on the meaning of the arrangement for an uncomfortable amount of time. I twisted my hands, began to sweat, played with my hair, and manically rubbed my forehead.

When we first started, I told Laura about waking up with the word Medjugorje in my head. She asked me if I knew of anyone, now deceased, who had revered the Virgin Mary or who would have been especially devout in worship of her. I wasn't sure. She went on to say that she saw a lot of spiritual strength on my mother's side of the family and she thought, perhaps, that a family member or a couple on my mother's side was trying to let me know that there was more to this world than it appeared. She stated that they were benevolent and were protecting me. She kept saying that they were "cute." She said she was hearing an accent and repeatedly heard the combination of the letters i and n. I was a little confused but thought if it was someone from my mother's side of the family, perhaps they were trying to communicate my mother's name, Jeanne. As a child of French-Canadian descent, my mother was called by her nickname, Little Jeanne. The French pronunciation would include i and n sounds. I could not think of any other correlations. I thought there was something comforting about the possibility that my family was trying to guide and protect me. Laura communicated a few other things to me during the reading, but I only half listened to her. Frankly, I was relieved when it was finished. Although I hadn't wanted the reading, I decided to focus on the possible good that it could bring. Perhaps it was part of the answer. If some deceased members of my family were trying to reach me, it was far better for me to focus on that as a plausible explanation, rather than having no explanation at all. The relief was short-lived. On the ride home I was an absolute wreck. I felt as though someone was in the car, hovering over me, and I kept looking over my shoulder at every stop sign. I was starting to feel that there was no escaping this craziness.

I went to Steve's apartment and told him what had happened. I said that I was still very uneasy about it. When I went to bed that night, however, I enjoyed another decent night of sound sleep. The next morning was Wednesday, and I woke up with another message. It came to me in the same way the previous morning's message had been received. No words, no voices—it was just there. This time the message was, *"You are diluting the messages by trying to figure out who is sending them."* I was startled by the relevancy of the message. It felt as though I had received a gentle scolding from my mother. At that moment, I immediately gained a full understanding of the message—it was in direct response to my search for answers through Laura. Although I was not yet clear about where to look for answers, I knew one thing for certain: I was no longer going to seek answers from psychics or mediums. I immediately destroyed all of the tape recordings of psychic readings and discarded all other materials I had collected from my previous psychic fairs. I was cleansing myself of any New Age connections, as I knew that wasn't the path for me. I also intrinsically understood that I needed to be less concerned about who or what was giving me these messages and instead dedicate more of my efforts to deciphering their meaning and determining what, if anything I was supposed to do.

This was also the day that I had arranged to see a therapist. I was apprehensive about telling her that my clock had changed on me and that I was getting messages from the spirit world. I had a feeling that if I told her this, she might refer me to a psychiatrist. I decided that I wouldn't tell her about the specific instances and instead would focus on the move to my new apartment and my general anxiety and obsessive thoughts. When we met, we talked about the fears I was experiencing related to my move. She acknowledged that some of my anxiety was normal, but some of it seemed irrational. She gave me specific things to do to make myself feel safer, such as getting stronger locks for the doors and securing my windows. She also gave me the name of an anti-anxiety workbook that had exercises to help manage my anxiety. I walked away from the session thinking that she had really done everything she could for me, but deep inside, I acknowledged that this was something that not even she could help me with, even if I'd told her everything. The problem was, I still wasn't sure who *could* help me.

After meeting with the therapist, I really wanted to talk to my mother. I knew that if anyone might understand some of the things I was going through, my mother would. Although both of my parents were active Catholics, my mother had always seemed to display a particularly firm and unshakeable faith. She had a strong belief in our religion and trusted in God. I called home that night, but my mother wasn't there. My father answered the phone, and I relayed the events to him. He listened intently and agreed that, indeed, it appeared that I was having some type of spiritual experience.

My mother called the next day, Thursday evening—the day before Steve and I were leaving on a trip to Ireland to visit his brother Gerry. My father had passed along what I'd told him, but she wanted more of the details. I started to tell her about everything, and when I got to the part about

Medjugorje, she said, "Amy! Medjugorje?"

I replied, "Yes, Mom, why?"

She said, "Did I tell you that I saw one of the children of Medjugorje?" My heart skipped a beat. I knew nothing about that; in fact, I knew very little about Medjugorje, having only heard of it for the first time when I received the message through an inner voice. My mother was astonished and went on to tell me that Ivanka, one of the children to whom Mary appeared, had visited a church near our home in Maine about three months earlier. Ivanka, who at the time was in her thirties, spoke to the people at the church about the apparitions of Mary and conveyed that each of the six children, who were known as visionaries, has a special mission in life. In addition to spreading Mary's messages, Ivanka's mission is to pray for families. My mother could not recall the exact details that Ivanka shared, but she did remember one key message that Mary delivered for the world through the visionaries: pray, pray, pray.

We also talked for a while about the fact that Ivanka appeared to be a regular person—a young woman, wife, and mother living a conventional daily existence. Yet she had been touched in a very special way by having the privilege of interacting with and speaking with the Mother of God. The consideration of Ivanka's life and this discussion with my mother was a tremendous relief. Although it might have seemed like a remote possibility and actually almost comical, I did briefly wonder if these happenings were calling me to some sort of deeper religious commitment, like becoming a nun. Hearing about Ivanka made me realize that people of all walks of life make their own unique contributions to the world and that becoming a nun wasn't the only way to respond to God. As we were concluding our conversation, I wondered out loud to my mother if I was, perhaps, supposed to meet Ivanka. I was, of course, searching for some answers, but my mother gave me a piece of advice. She said, "These things are not things that you can plan. You have to just go with it, and you will know what you need to do when the time is right." I welcomed the advice and felt a renewed sense of energy. I felt normal again; I was in the best spirits I had been in since the occurrences began.

PLANTING
THE SEED

"Dear children, this year how much seed I have sown. I desire that you, dear children, be my flower from that seed. Be my flower. Live my message. Pray for peace. Pray together with your mother Mary for peace. Thank you for having responded to my call."[1]

~Mary's Message of September 8, 2006~

Four
Golden Cross

On Friday, Steve's father, Eugene (or Gene, as we call him), picked us up at my apartment to take us to the airport. During the ride, Steve suggested that I update his father on all of the things that had been happening to me. So I told him the drama that had unfolded over the past couple of weeks, up to and including the conversation I'd had the previous evening with my mother. "It's so unbelievable that my mother met one of the children of Medjugorje," I declared to Gene, "especially since it was only months ago."

I wasn't quite prepared for what he said next. "Medjugorje? I just finished reading a book about Medjugorje." Chills streamed throughout my body, and Steve and I looked at each other in disbelief. Gene went on to tell us that a few weeks earlier, he had been looking through a bin of used books at the grocery store and found one titled *Medjugor-*

je, The Message—which he then purchased for twenty-five cents! He said the book was written by a Protestant journalist who wrote about messages sent by the Virgin Mary. The author had gone to Medjugorje, and his experiences there had changed him radically. The book is about his personal journey and how it impacted his life. Gene offered to lend it to me if I wanted to read it.

Steve and I immediately recognized that *Medjugorje, The Message* was one of the two books I was considering reading from the list Steve pulled together from his Internet research. We sat stunned and speechless for a moment while we tried to absorb the serendipity of the situation. Then Steve proclaimed, "Well, I'm pretty sure we just found out which book you should be reading!" I became very excited to start reading it, and felt somewhat disappointed that it wasn't in my immediate possession. Steve and I later talked about buying a copy while we were on vacation, but we agreed that I should wait and borrow it from his father when we returned from our trip, given there may be something inherently special about his particular copy.

We arrived in Ireland safely and went immediately to Steve's brother's house, where we decided to take a nap after the long flight. I awoke from my nap to the sounds of children laughing and playing behind Gerry's apartment. I could tell that they were close by, but I looked out the window and was unable to see them. At first, I wondered if the sounds of children were real or perhaps only an extension of the dreams I had back at home. But the sounds that trailed in the distance were different. They were so normal. They lacked the brilliance and joy that I'd heard, and even somehow felt, in my previous dreams. I did not understand what the sounds represented, but they lingered within me in a mysterious and curious way. In contrast, these earthly sounds seemed depressing. Although I knew I was experiencing increased stress as a result of the events, I was, at the same time, beginning to long for more of the supernatural.

Steve's brother, Gerry, had to work during the first day of our visit, but we met him in the early evening. We made our way to several Irish pubs, chatting and catching up along the way. In the midst of this, I was still extremely nervous—so much so that I was actually afraid to go into the restrooms by myself for fear that something strange would happen to me while I was in there. I did not yet tell anyone this, but I was terrified every time I had to be alone. I was terrified to close my eyes and go to sleep, even if Steve was in the same room. When I was awake, however, and with Steve and Gerry or other people, I thought that nothing could possibly happen to me. At one point in that first evening, Steve sensed that I was having an extremely difficult time and suggested that I tell Gerry what had transpired, beginning with the clock incident. He knew that Gerry had dealt with some psychic-type experiences in his life and would understand. I nervously started to divulge all the events that had taken place thus far. Gerry listened intently and responded supportively. "All the things that happened seemed to be good," he told me. "You should be happy that it was good energy and seemed positive."

I tried in earnest to take his advice, but when we returned to his house, it was very clear that I was still extremely anxious. Gerry was quite surprised at how tense I was. After the long flight and time zone changes, he thought I should have been exhausted, not wound up.

We discussed why I was afraid, but I didn't understand it myself, especially because my conversation with my mother had done so much to calm me. Gerry suggested that I just relax and "go with it"—exactly what my mother had said. Then, Gerry changed the subject and asked me if I minded talking about marriage and children. I said that Steve and I were very open about it. We'd been dating for about a year at this point, and were serious about our relationship. Gerry pressed Steve about his views on the subject, and Steve expressed that he did not want to bring children into this world.

"The world is a terrible place," he said adamantly, "and it isn't fair to bring an innocent child into it. Adopting children makes sense, though, because they're already here and need parents or loving people to take care of them."

I completely agreed with his perspective on adoption. In fact, we'd had many conversations in the past about it and agreed that we would be ideal candidates to adopt children. We both agreed that it could be a powerful, positive step to care for a child or children who needed a family, yet I was surprised to learn during the conversation with Gerry that Steve was actually opposed to bringing life into the world. I found it difficult to understand his reasoning for not wanting to have biological children—it seemed contradictory to other aspects of his personality. He was loving, kind, and outgoing. He had a positive outlook on life and a passion for being active and embracing opportunities.

Although I felt a little uncomfortable asking him this trite question, I said, "Do you ever look at me and feel that you love me so much that one day you would like to create a child together?"

He hesitated, as if processing something, but did not directly answer my question.

"Your view bewilders me," I continued. "And it surprises me, especially because you've been the one who's been sustaining me, the one who has faith that everything going on with me is good and is going to work out. How can you be so certain about a positive outcome for me but at the same time hold such a fatalist view of the world?"

Steve looked somewhat stressed, or maybe even disturbed. I could tell that he was thinking deeply about something. He looked down and suddenly became very emotional. I wasn't sure what he was experiencing at that moment, but when he looked up I saw tears in his eyes. He had started to cry and began nodding his head. "Yes," he said, as he looked directly at me. "Someday, I want to have a child."

As Steve was in the midst of this very emotional experience, I could only stare at his forehead, where the most remarkable sight emerged. A large golden cross began to glow over the bridge of his nose and on his forehead. The cross mesmerized and entranced me. I felt a warm, calming sensation engulf me, and I was immediately suspended in time as I stared at the cross. It was gentle, peaceful, and comforting. It never once occurred to me to ask Gerry if he could see it. I was simply enveloped by it. Steve stood up then, and as we hugged, I told him about what I'd seen on his forehead. Both Steve and Gerry were amazed by my vivid description of the golden cross. I asked Steve what he'd been thinking about as he was crying—when the cross appeared. He explained that he'd experienced an epiphany. Something just clicked within him, and in that precise moment, he understood that willfully bringing a child into this world was the truest act of faith he could possibly display to God. Gerry and I now were very moved too, and we all hugged.

Gerry told us how blessed we were and how much love there was in the room. He smiled and said, "See? You have to get married and have kids." Then Gerry looked at me and said, "You have your answer." I knew he was referring to my dreams and experiences. Although we knew there were many more pieces to this puzzle, we all concluded that the occurrences—the dream, the clock, the book, the cross, and other events—were not for me alone; they were for both Steve and me.

Five

A Choir of Angels

The next night, Steve and I met Gerry at a local pub after he had attended a memorial service for a friend who had died two years earlier. His deceased friend's parents were present—the mother looked over at us and smiled genuinely—and many of his friends were there, too.

A little while later, I had to make my way to the restroom, which I was dreading, especially because it was in the basement. As I walked over to the stairs I almost ran into the mother. She looked at me and smiled again. I felt sad when I looked at her but also thought that she must be happy to see all of the people who were present for her son's memorial. When I entered the restroom, I saw that the doors to the three stalls were open, and I quickly realized that I was the only one in the room. My heart began to thump nervously. I had a sinking feeling in my stomach—I was in the basement of the pub all by myself, with no one else around. It made me feel exposed and vulnerable. Without the perceived protection of some other human being, I felt susceptible to more paranormal intrusions. I stepped into the restroom stall—it was so tiny I could barely fit in and actually had difficulty turning around to close the door behind me. I wondered why it was so small and complained silently about the impracticality of the construction. Within fifteen to twenty seconds, I heard the bathroom door open and the sound of two girls conversing and laughing. I immediately felt relief that I was no longer alone. It did not matter who was with me, just that someone was. My protective shield was restored, and I was convinced that no supernatural force was going to play games with me. I listened to the girls' voices as they laughed and giggled. When I emerged from the stall, I expected to see the other two stall doors closed, with each girl in her own stall, yet one stall was open and one was closed. Both girls were together in one stall, I concluded, and that was curious to me, as the stalls were so tiny. The doors were full length, from ceiling to floor, so I wasn't certain that they were in there together, but I heard their chatter and the sound of two distinct voices. Something about the situation struck me as odd, but I could not determine exactly what it was. I turned to the sink, washed my hands, and then pressed the button on the electric hand dryer. Warm air began to flow out of the dryer, and its drone covered the girls' chatter, at least momentarily. In the next few seconds I was startled by the sound that came next from the stall—it was high-pitched, very loud singing, though I could not recognize any words. *How bizarre*, I thought. *Why would these girls be singing at the top of their lungs?* Then I realized something even more

46

remarkable. The voices were singing in absolutely perfect unison. They sounded like a choir of angels. I didn't know what was going on in there, but I was absolutely certain that I heard angels singing. I made my way up the stairway very quickly and rejoined Steve at the gathering. I was distracted for the rest of the evening, thinking about the sounds that I had heard, but I didn't mention anything to Steve about what I had been through.

Over the next day, I replayed those moments in the bathroom over and over in my head and contemplated a variety of explanations. Maybe it had something to do with the individual who was being memorialized. Maybe that was his way of expressing that he was happy that people had gathered together in his name. Perhaps I was somehow a receptacle for his message. Or maybe it was just a figment of my imagination. Maybe those girls were not really there, and I only imagined the choir of angels.

Steve and I decided to rent a car and travel to the west coast of Ireland. We made our way to Galway, and then decided to head southwest toward the beautiful Cliffs of Moher. Unfortunately, I was navigating; I didn't realize that taking us to Limerick for the night would put us significantly off course from the cliffs. We checked into our hotel and went downstairs to relax in the lounge. I was sitting on a bench next to Steve when I suddenly felt shivers through my entire body. I'd heard many times that a full-body shiver indicates that a ghost is passing through your body. I decided to move to a chair, though I didn't tell Steve why I moved. Steve then scooted down the bench to where I had been sitting. Within a couple of seconds, he said, "I just had one of those chills."

"I just experienced that exact same exact thing!" I said, astounded. "That's why I moved." This was downright creepy, and I once again felt that there was no escape from this ongoing drama.

We left the lounge and went back to the hotel room to go to sleep. Steve, of course, had no problem falling asleep. I, on the other hand, was still terrified; all my nerve endings were on alert. I was so afraid of what I might see in the dark or what might come to me in the night that I simply could not sleep. I turned on the television and tried to distract my mind. I even counted sheep, but nothing brought me any relief from my insomnia. The more I tried to sleep, the harder it became. Then, around 2:00 in the morning, the group of people staying next door returned to their room. They were loud and boisterous and appeared to be having a party. They were laughing, talking, and playing music. Under normal circumstances, I would have been highly annoyed at such a disruption. In this case, however, I actually felt relieved. The rumble of loud, chaotic voices actually brought me a strange sense of comfort. Once again, I thought that if those people were next door, just behind the wall, so close and so full of activity, then nothing could happen to me. As that thought ran through my head, I heard a Beatles song coming from our TV. It was "The Long and Winding Road." The music distracted me from the noise next door and turned my attention to the words. What happened after that seemed to occur instantly. As soon as I heard the lyrics "lead me to your door," I was enveloped by a majestic sound that surged through me with a sweeping force. Once again, it appeared to be angels. They were singing loudly, beautifully, and harmoniously! As their heavenly melody swelled, it drowned out all other sounds, and I felt a rushing sensation, as if I was literally being whisked out of my bed and into the vast but comforting space of the universe. I sensed that there were stars all around me in a deep blue sky. The next thing I knew, it was morning and I was waking from my slumber.

We had only one more day in Ireland after that, and there were no more sensational events. Fortunately, it gave me time to reflect upon the angels and their significance. Although I could not fully comprehend their intervention, it was clear that they had been sent to provide some sort of comfort to me during a time of distress.

Overall, the entire experience in Ireland was extremely mysterious. It seemed that everywhere I looked, the image of the cross appeared. I would become acutely aware of the outline of the cross imbedded in almost everything I saw—in the cut glass of windows, in the latticework of fences, and along the sides of the roads. I recall walking in Dublin with Gerry and Steve one evening. As we turned a corner, I saw a statue of the Virgin Mary holding Jesus in her arms. It startled me, as I had never seen a religious statue like that in a main area of a large city. Seeing images of Mary and Jesus in Ireland is not unique, but the images were very powerful. They filled me with a sense of both mystery and fear. While my recent experiences were beautiful, I was probably still fearful because there was so much going on around me that was unexplained. I knew in my heart that it all somehow led back to Jesus and Mary.

Six

The Mystery of 7:24

We left Ireland after nine days and returned to New York. Steve's father picked us up at the airport, and we had much to tell him about our trip. As we got closer to home, we decided to call Steve's mother to see if she wanted to go out to dinner with us. We picked her up and went to a local restaurant, where we talked about our trip over dinner. During the meal, however, I kept feeling that there was a presence hovering over my left shoulder. In fact, I tried to physically wave this presence away from me. Silently, I communicated to it and told it to leave me alone for a while, because I really did not want to deal with any of its games; I needed a break. The presence stayed with me as I tried to focus on the conversation at the dinner table.

I was tired from our travels and was getting anxious to go home and get settled, but for some reason, Steve's mother was eating painstakingly slow. I glanced down at my watch; it was close to 8:00. She finally finished her food and we left the restaurant. Steve's parents dropped us off at my apartment. After we had been there for a little while, I looked at the clock in the living room—the same one that had changed its time a few weeks back. It read 7:25. *That's odd*, I thought. *We left the restaurant at 8:00.* I went into my bedroom to check the clock in there; it read 8:25. I walked back into the living room and asked Steve to look at the clock and tell me what time it was. He said, "7:25." Then I told him to go into the bedroom and compare it to the time there.

He knew where I was going with this and said, "Maybe it's stuck or something." Even so, he went into the bedroom. "You're right, hon," he called to me. "I know what you mean now."

I was relieved and excited—someone else finally had seen what I had seen that first night when I was alone. It felt good to be validated. "It's so amazing that you, too, have now observed the phenomena," I said excitedly. "What do you think it might mean?"

Steve looked at me, bleary-eyed and fatigued. I had relied so heavily on him over the past couple of weeks by telling him every minute detail of my experiences. Although he had intently listened to me and was fully supportive, it was taxing on him, and I had drained his energy. Now, with jet lag setting in, he did not want to talk about any of these mysteries—and that was hard for me to understand. I thought he would be as amazed as I was, but it didn't really seem to faze him. We said good night, and I went to bed, leaving the clock in the living room untouched—I wasn't about to adjust the time.

Steve fell asleep on the couch in the living room, and the next morning when I awoke, he asked me to look closely at the clock and tell him what time it was. I told him it said 7:25.

"No, look *very* closely at it," he said.

When I looked more closely, I realized that the clock was actually stopped at 7:24.

"Well, technically," I told him, "its 7:24. Why?"

"Guess what time I woke up this morning?" he said. I looked at him with excited curiosity and awaited his next comment. "7:24," he said.

This time it was my turn to be the skeptic. "Of course," I said. "You checked the time on this clock—and it's stuck."

"No," he said. "I looked at that one," and pointed to the clock on the Video Cassette Recorder (VCR) on the television stand. This clock was digital and displayed an exact time. Steve went on to describe how he had awakened unusually early. He always sleeps late and after our taxing travel back to the US, had expected to wake up mid-day. "I don't know why but for some reason I woke up instantly this morning. I felt groggy from the trip and was really tired so I looked at the clock to see what time it was." That's when he noticed the display on the VCR read 7:24.

Knowing that the other clock had stopped again the previous evening and suddenly waking up to the same exact time, Steve now clearly recognized that we were both meant to witness this phenomenon together. Steve had powerfully reaffirmed what I already knew. Whatever the meaning of this message, it was meant for both of us. Neither of us could interpret the significance of it, but we agreed that we

The mysterious clock stuck at 7:24.

were being given some sign. Perhaps it was for the future and we would need to wait for whatever it was to unfold.

That night when I went to bed, I contemplated using the earplugs that Gerry had given me in Ireland—both he and Steve snored so loudly that I would have been up all night without them. I have never liked the idea of using earplugs to close off my hearing, but on this night I decided to put them in once more so that Steve's snoring would not disrupt my sleep. I was still having problems relaxing at night and wasn't sleeping well. I gently inserted the plugs into my ears and then shifted my head on the pillow to find a comfortable resting position. I could vaguely hear Steve snoring, so I pushed the plugs in a little deeper until I could no longer hear any sound. I closed my eyes, and my body began to relax. Within seconds, I heard what sounded like knocking. It startled me, but I lay still and listened carefully. Where was this coming from? The knocking became louder, and suddenly, my heart beat faster. I did not move a muscle, but I had a shocking realization as fear enveloped my body: I had just put in the earplugs and had effectively blocked out all sound. Yet with intensifying clarity, I could now hear a deep knocking, and it sounded as if it was emanating from the basement. *How was this possible?* I asked myself, as I lay stiff in the bed, paralyzed with alarm. Then, something triggered within me, like the night when the clock first changed. I became determined to face the fear that was once again taking a grip on me. I realized that I could not shut out the overwhelming auditory sensations so I told myself to relax and just take in everything. As I relaxed and opened myself up, the sounds became clearer. At first, I could hear only the faint sounds of a woman weeping in the background, but the sound of banging became extremely clear. It seemed as if it was directly below my bed, and it became evident to me that it was actually the sound of someone being whipped! Although I never saw anything during this experience, I somehow knew that it was a man doing the whipping, and I knew that there were the muffled cries of a woman (I sensed it was a mother) in the background. I could not figure out, who, however, was being whipped. There were no sounds or cries from the person being whipped—just silence—but my instincts told me that it was a child. Soon, everything came together for me—I was able to feel that a man was whipping a child, and that the mother and perhaps some other women were on-looking and weeping in the background—my heart sank again, and I immediately began to pray with all of my heart and soul. I prayed with more fervor and intensity than I had ever prayed in my entire life. I asked God to please forgive this soul, this spirit, for perpetrating this act. I prayed for God's forgiveness for this soul's horrible deed. I prayed the Our Father and the Hail Mary. I did not know what else to pray, but the prayers just came out, like the words to a favorite song from long ago. Within about thirty seconds, I noticed something astonishing. The sounds of the whipping and crying slowly began to fade. I kept praying, and the sounds faded, and faded, and faded, until they were completely gone. Silence. I lay there for a minute in shock. My prayers had helped. My prayers had made a difference.

It was absolutely remarkable. I took my earplugs out and placed them on the table. I had not been dreaming; this had occurred in a waking state. Although my eyes had been closed, I was completely awake for this incredible auditory experience. Having been so confused before about what was happening to me, I now thought that perhaps the purpose of all that I had been going through may have been to lead me to this—the development of an ability that I could use to help release a soul from being "stuck." Maybe it was this soul that had changed my clock or popped the cork in the bottle. Maybe this was an abusive soul, or maybe it was the soul of a child who was abused and needed prayers. Whatever the case, I was convinced that I had solved the problem with all of the things that had been happening to me. In some ways, I guess I expected things to be over. The next morning

SEASON OF THE ROSE

when I got up, I have to admit that I was sure that the clock stuck on 7:24 would have changed, but it had not.

That night, I traveled to Philadelphia on a business trip. On the plane ride down, I noticed a beautiful rainbow. It made me feel spiritual and connected, but I still wasn't completely at ease. When I checked into my hotel room and tried to settle in, I was definitely nervous, as this was the first night since all of these things started happening that I would be completely alone. I kept looking over my shoulder and was very uneasy. I picked up the phone beside the bed to ask for a wake-up call in the morning. The phone was dead. I put it down and picked it up again. Same thing. Once again, I pleaded with whatever presence was with me to "give me a break." I said out loud that I did not want to be bothered, that I was tired. I spoke in a very annoyed tone, but it was also a plea. I put the phone down and picked it back up again. Thankfully, this time it worked. Once again, I felt as though my request had been honored. I called the front desk and asked for a 7:30 wake-up call for the next day. I got into bed and managed to get to sleep. When the phone rang in the morning, I sat up in bed to take my wake-up call. When I hung up the phone, I looked over at the clock—and it was exactly 7:24.

I was very distracted that day at work. It was hard to concentrate, as my mind kept wandering to the important events of my personal life. As I sat in my meeting, high above the city of Philadelphia, I looked out to the towering building next door. I could see images of crosses as part of the structure of the building. I stared at the sparkling windows as the sun's light illuminated the shape of crosses in the engineered structure of the windows. I tried to suppress the outlines of crosses so that I could stay focused on my work—the flickering images distracted me, and I knew I had to be attentive to the meeting. At one of our breaks, I went into the restroom; there were several women in there. As I was drying my hands with a paper towel, I heard the door open and several more women walked in. I was startled by the sound of a high-pitched squeaky door, and at the same time the door opened, I heard my name called out in a elongated, melodic, angelic beckoning: "*Amy.*" I turned toward the doorway to see who had called to me. Some of my coworkers were there but were engrossed in their own conversation. They walked right in, not even looking at me, and continued talking to one another. None of them had called my name.

That night, I flew home and called Steve's father, asking if I could borrow the book on Medjugorje—I was anxious to read it. I drove over to his house to get it on my way to work that next morning and was excited to finally have the book in my hands. It was as if it contained some great secret, and I was somehow set in motion to decode it. I started reading it that very morning while waiting in traffic at the red lights on my way to work. During lunch, I sat in my car in the parking lot, devouring its contents.

I was highly distracted at work and could not wait to go home to continue reading. At the same time, I was still very distraught about what was going on and did not feel that I could fully cope with the magnitude and uncertainty of what was happening to me. I cried in my office, hoping no one would notice. I didn't even feel like eating. I called my friend Suzie that day and shared my story with her. She was astonished and supportive, yet her sincere words of encouragement could not allay my fears.

The next day, I called my mother to give her an update. I told her about the book, the cross on Steve's forehead in Ireland, the choir of angels, and about the sounds of the whipping. It was at this moment—when I was telling my mother about the sounds of the whipping in my apartment and as I was just about to tell her about my theory of saving some soul—that I had a great realization. It occurred to me, for the first time, that the sounds of the child being whipped and the mother crying were not what I had thought. I had not saved a soul from damnation. I had not freed anyone. I had not solved my problems. What I immediately understood was that the sounds signified something much greater and much more profound. I trembled as I heard the words escape from my mouth. "Mom," I said, "I know what those sounds were, what they represent. You're not going to believe this, but they were the sounds of Jesus Christ being whipped." I could hardly believe what I was saying. But it all came together in an instant: the silent child; the mother weeping in the background; the other women in the background; the prayers. It was all too much for me to take in. To say that I had an epiphany was an understatement. I was overwhelmed. I just knew, somewhere inside, that this was what I had experienced. I needed time to think about my revelation, and I abruptly ended the call with my mother, promising to call again soon.

For the first time since all of the occurrences began to unfold over the past month, I finally understood that there was a thread to all of it—being startled awake out of a dead sleep at my apartment; being whisked into slumber by angels; being called by name by an angelic choir; having a book on Mary's visit to earth placed immediately before me. It all started to crystallize that something divine was occurring. I did not know why I had been chosen to experience this, but I was certain that there was, indeed, heavenly intervention in my life. I had tried, unsuccessfully, to find comfort in other human beings and in the things of this world that I knew. When I was scared to be in the bathroom by myself, I looked for the girls to provide safety. When I was exhausted and needed to sleep, I tried to find solace in the boisterous neighbors in the hotel room. When I noticed crosses in the reflection of the building in Philadelphia, I tried to suppress the visions by focusing on my work. Yet each time that I sought the relief from the things of this world, something remarkable happened. Angels were there to comfort me. They called out to me by name and sang to me. They beckoned me and whisked me away from my troubles. As surprising as it was, I now knew with certainty that there was only one place for me to go—and that was directly to Jesus. It was Jesus, and Him alone, to whom I needed to go. Yet like everything else, this was incredibly perplexing.

At this moment in my life, I was what some people have called a convenient Catholic. Although I was born and raised in a Roman Catholic family, received the expected sacraments of the church (Baptism, First Holy Communion, and Confirmation), believed that Jesus Christ was our Savior, and went to church on major holidays such as Easter and Christmas and sometimes in between, I wasn't a practicing Catholic—I didn't attend Mass regularly or live according to the church's teachings. I had moved to Connecticut in 1998 and probably had gone to Mass only a handful of times over the previous three years. In fact, I wasn't even sure where many of the Catholic churches were located in my area. Fortunately, I was aware of one church. I passed it every day on my work commute. On this night, I decided to stop there on my way home.

When I arrived at the church, the doors were locked. Determined to get in, I walked into the parish office. I was almost in tears when I asked a woman in the office if I could get into the church. She was so wonderful and let me in the side entrance. I kneeled in the front pew. I had never in my life been in a church all by myself. There I was, alone, kneeling before Jesus, and crying and shaking. I cannot remember all the things I said to Jesus at this time, but I do know that I told Him that I was scared and that I was finally figuring out that He was the one to whom I needed to come. No one else could help me understand why these things were happening to me, and no one else could solve the mystery of 7:24. I don't know how long I stayed there; I don't think it was very long, but by the time I was ready to leave, I had relaxed to such a point that my body had stopped shaking.

TAKING ROOT

"Dear children! I desire to call you to grow in love. A flower is not able to grow normally without water. So also you, dear children, are not able to grow without God's blessing. From day to day you need to seek His blessing so you will grow normally and perform all your actions in union with God. Thank you for having responded to my call."[1]

~Mary's Message of April 10, 1986~

Seven

The Main Messages

Over the next couple of days after my epiphany, I contin-
ued reading and re-reading the book *Medjugorje, The Mes-*
sage with incredible interest and focus. I found myself so
enthralled with its contents that I eagerly turned each new
page to learn more. Prior to reading the book, I had only
a superficial understanding of the phenomenon at Medjugorje. I knew that six children in a small village in what is
now Bosnia-Herzegovina reported seeing visions of Mary,
the mother of Jesus. She appeared to them and provided
messages for them to convey to the world. I didn't know
much beyond that, and I interpreted the word "children"
very literally. Then, as I read the book, I learned the six were
children at the time Mary first appeared to them in 1981;
today, they are middle-aged adults. The visions of Mary actually had commenced twenty years earlier. It was astound-

ing. How was it that I was getting messages related to Mary, as these children had? And why now, more than twenty years after Mary first had begun appearing in Medjugorje? How was I involved or connected to this, and what was the significance? This newfound temporal context merely heightened the intensity with which I sought more answers. I hastily read through the details and learned that although the messages began twenty years ago, they still occur in the present day. Mary still appears in some fashion to all of the original six children, or visionaries, delivering her urgent messages for the world to return to God.

The following excerpt from the book, *Medjugorje, The Message,* outlines the events with astounding clarity. Although it primarily gives insight into the initial events, the key themes and most important points are represented here. The author, Wayne Weible, pulls from his own original newspaper articles that he published on the Medjugorje phenomenon to describe the following events:

MIRACLE AT MEDJUGORJE

Part 1: The Apparitions

December 14, 1985

In the next four weeks of December, I am going to try to give as accurate an account as possible of an event allegedly occurring in a small nondescript village in the hills of central Yugoslavia. It is a supernatural religious event and is therefore bound to be viewed in a

skeptical sense by many; in fact, that the area
is heavily Catholic will add to that skepticism.
Obviously, if I personally did not believe there was something important happening there, I would not be writing about
it. However, let me say from the outset, it
is not an attempt to convert anyone to Catholicism, since I myself am not Catholic; it
is also not an attempt to convert anyone to
a belief in God. That is for the individual to
determine, based on information and needs.
I offer it simply as information timely to the
Christmas season.

* * *

For the past four and a half years
now, Medjugorje (pronounced Med-jew-gor-
yay), a small village in the mountain area of
central Yugoslavia, has attracted worldwide
attention as the place where the mother of Jesus, Mary, is reported to be appearing almost
daily to six young teenagers. As I write this,
the apparitions reportedly continue every
day. Despite the government attempts to dis-
credit the apparitions and to make the visits
to the site difficult, millions have been and
continue to come to the site to see for themselves what is happening. Yugoslavia is, of
course, a communist country, which does
not recognize any religion or the existence of

God. Yet theirs is a heavily Catholic population that is grudgingly allowed to worship within their churches.

According to the children—called seers or visionaries—the message of the Blessed Virgin is simple and direct; she is appearing to the seers to tell the world of the urgency to return to the ways of God, to convert their lives to peace with God and with their fellow man. She is to give each seer 10 messages or "secrets" of happenings that will occur in the near future. These messages will be visible signs to mankind that the apparitions at Medjugorje are real and that the conversion back to God must be started now. When she has stopped appearing to the youths—a time known only to them—a permanent sign will be left at Medjugorje. It will lead to many healings and conversions in the short time left before the messages will become a reality.

The way to conversion is prayer and fasting, according to the seers. Since the apparitions began on June 21, 1981, the seers spend as many as six hours or more in daily prayer. They also fast up to three times a week on bread and water only.

The range in age of the six young people at Medjugorje is noteworthy in view of the skepticism of such an occurrence. When the apparitions began, one was only ten years old, another was fifteen, three were sixteen, and one was seventeen. Four are girls and two are boys.

Weible goes on to briefly describe each of the six visionaries. Their names are Mirjana Dragicevic, Maria Pavlovic, Vicka Ivankovic, Ivanka Ivankovic, Ivan Dragicevic, and Jakov Colo. Overall, he describes them as mostly average teenagers with nothing exceptional about their backgrounds or situations, other than a growing devotion to Mary and religion. He mentions the youngest, Jakov, who was only ten at the time of the apparitions, writing, "Comparing him to, say, our own children or brothers of this age, it would normally be highly improbable that he would go to church for two and three hours of prayer every single day, in winter and summer, in bad weather and good, and do this for well over four years, simply to make believe that he is seeing a holy apparition from God."[1]

My heart and head swirled with a flurry of emotions—disbelief, confusion, fear, and uncertainty. I'd been living an average life with little or no concern for the future, for humanity, or for the world, and in an instant, my life was turned upside down as I became somehow entangled in a worldwide spiritual phenomenon that called for a return to God. As I read the book, there were moments when I was so overwhelmed that I literally felt sick to my stomach. I learned about the call to quickly turn my life over to God.

What I discovered wasn't just that Mary was appearing and telling mankind to open its heart to God; she was helping us to understand how to do so—and that is what terrified me. How was I going to do that? How was I going to change my behaviors and give up things on which I had never even questioned myself? My fascination with the story turned to fear when I realized that not only the visionaries but the whole community in Medjugorje had taken up many different practices and exercises recommended by Mary as ways to draw closer to God. For example, they began to practice an old tradition of strictly fasting on bread and water on Wednesdays and Fridays, and they attended hours and hours of prayer services daily. Some people even demonstrated significant acts of repentances by doing things such as walking miles in their bare feet until they bled, and hiking up mountains barefoot to give glory to God and to repent for certain behaviors.

Opening my heart to God was one thing, but why did it need to be so extreme? All of this was just too much for me to take in. I was in a major state of internal strife and conflict. I was drawn to this story with an insatiable interest and yet, at the same time I did not relate at all to it. I knew that I was a part of it, but at times I wanted nothing to do with a lifestyle so different from my own. I perceived these visionaries and villagers as religious fanatics. Why would anyone walk in their bare feet until they bled as a way to give honor to God? How could these people fast on bread and water every week? How did they have time for hours and hours of daily prayer? To me, they were living in a distant world in a manner that was truly foreign to me, one that held no resemblance to my American life. I was a young, up-and-coming professional, living in a land of opportunity, and fulfilling my career and personal goals—traveling, dating, playing, and self-actualizing. I believed that getting the most out of life was what it was all about. Achievement, goal-orientation, self-fulfillment, and the pursuit of individual dreams were my constant focus. How, then, did this story of Mary and this village relate to me? The questions nagged at me. I wanted to turn away and have everything return to the way it was before I had even heard the word Medjugorje. I was distraught, confused, and alone. There was really no one who could possibly understand the turmoil I was experiencing.

By the time I finished reading the book, I was consumed by the magnitude, seriousness, and urgency of these messages. Although I initially rebuked the actions and behaviors of the visionaries and villagers, I instinctively knew that the story and their ways—definitely influenced by visions from Mary—were too great to ignore or disregard. Although I could not fully understand their way of life, I also knew I was being called toward the very messages emanating from their village. The notion that I was somehow linked to heavenly messages from God and Mary regarding the current and future state of the world still seemed incomprehensible—and impossible. Yet I knew that what I had experienced was real. Supernatural events were happening in my life, and they led me directly and unequivocally to the heart of Medjugorje and to Mary's messages for the world.

I continued to be impressed by the timing of the outreach. I wasn't even a teenager when Mary first reportedly appeared to the visionaries. Here I was, at thirty-two, hearing for the first time a secret so miraculous that it seemed the whole world should know about it. During the first twenty years of the apparitions, it was reported that more than twenty million pilgrims had journeyed to the village.[2] How was it that every Catholic, if not those of other religions, did not know about this amazing set of circumstances? With Mary's status in the church, it would seem that all Catholics would have a fundamental awareness of Medjugorje. Most important, however, if the messages were urgent twenty years ago, what did that mean for the present day? Were we on the cusp of something that none of us could have imagined or prepared for? I had no answers; I only knew that I was going to take this seriously. Once I determined the exact path that had been set before me, there was no doubt that I would follow it.

After finishing the book, I fed my intense appetite for Medjugorje by consuming a variety of information—I visited websites, read more books, watched videotapes, and talked with people who had traveled there or studied it in order to build my own understanding of what was happening. Specifically, I learned that Mary first had appeared in the village on a hillside known natively as Podbrdo, or Apparition Hill. She appeared as a radiant, glowing figure and addressed the children. She told the children that the world was in need of peace, and she called for humanity to come back to God. She identified herself as the "Blessed Virgin Mary" and called herself the "Queen of Peace." She specifically told the children that "Peace must rule between man and God and also among the people."[3]

Mary's appearance created a tidal wave of activity in the remote village. As a small community of Catholics living under the strong arm of Communist leaders, having six children declare that they were seeing the Mother of God was almost outrageous. They were chased after by authorities and their families reportedly threatened with harm. The children, however, never wavered from their claims that Mary was appearing to them, despite the fact that they were, at times, subject to strange tests—lights were shined in their eyes, and their brain activity was monitored during the apparitions. The children held firm that they see and interact with Mary in a special way. At first, the children had visions at the hill. Eventually, they occurred in the church and in other places. Early on, the whole community gathered around daily, waiting to hear Mary's messages relayed through the children. All of her messages focused on five key themes that are applicable to the world: seeking peace for all mankind; having faith; converting one's heart and ways to God; praying unceasingly; and fasting regularly.[4] These same messages and the miraculous visits continue to this day. We also know that she reserved ten secrets for each of the visionaries; they were told not to reveal them until an appointed time. Reportedly, these secrets have to do with the visionaries themselves, the church, and the future of the entire world. Yet as fascinating and sensational as the secrets might be, Mary reminds us not to focus on them. Rather, she tells us to work on converting our hearts. In fact, she says that we have the power to change events and the course of the world, particularly through prayer. During one of her early appearances, she stated, "You have forgotten that with prayer and fasting you can ward off wars, suspend the laws of nature."[5]

Like a consummate teacher, Mary also provides very specific suggestions for spiritual exercise, such as attending

Holy Mass, praying the rosary, and going to confession.[6] The villagers and others who travel there make earnest efforts to change their lives in accordance with these messages. Like the people in the remote village, I, too, felt called to action. I began to demonstrate the first true acts of faith in my life as I practiced some of the recommendations, such as praying, fasting, and attending Mass. I did not necessarily feel close to God during this time, and I didn't even know where the road might lead, but I knew I had to make an effort to apply what I had learned.

Eight

Seeking Spiritual Relief

As part of this new spiritual journey, I deeply yearned for a more foundational spiritual direction. Born and raised a Catholic, I naturally turned to the only religious construct I knew, Catholicism. There were a couple of obstacles to overcome, however, as I sought out spiritual "relief" and direction. First, I very quickly learned that I knew almost nothing about my faith. As I reflected upon my religious experiences and involvement, I realized that I had mostly spent my childhood and early adult years simply going through the motions. Although I had attended Mass every Sunday with my family and was instructed in the basics of the faith, I either had not fully understood or had not retained the basic principles. What did it really mean to be baptized? Why did I kneel in the pews in church on cue? What had it really meant when I received Holy Communion at Mass for all of these years? In essence, what did it mean to be Catholic—or even a Christian?

The second major obstacle was this: once I started to understand my faith, I initially resisted almost everything that I heard. Maybe the issue was that I had, indeed, heard the teachings for all those years, but I'd blatantly chosen to ignore them. And I was very comfortable ignoring them, because it allowed me to perpetuate a life of perceived freedom, where I choose my own destiny and shape my own direction, morality, and existence. Therefore, I did not need the church. After all, like many disillusioned Catholics, I believed that the church teachings were unnecessarily harsh, conservative, punitive, behind the times, and not applicable to me. I could not understand, for example, why we had to confess our sins to a priest. He is just human, too. Furthermore, the word *sin* seemed archaic. Who uses that word anymore? Certainly no one differentiates between mortal sins and venial sins. Why be so nitpicky? God forgives us for everything, right? And what about not using any artificial birth control and not having premarital relations? What about all the wonderful people impacted by divorce? Why should the church have jurisdiction over such private matters? The questions went on and on, but I was certain about one thing: the Catholic Church had no right to tell me how to live.

When I thought in depth about these issues, my internal protests turned to anger. There seemed to be so many rules. I just could not seem to accept Catholicism as a way to true freedom. It seemed just the opposite. It just didn't feel right. At times, I was downright obstinate and refused to believe that God actually expected us to live by such rigid standards. I often thought that the church wasn't modern; it wasn't keeping pace with the world. Many of these guide-lines were written hundreds and even thousands of years ago. They could not possibly be applicable in this day and age. Yet the more I dug in, the more I discovered how very little I understood about the objective teachings, and I un-derstood even less about why the church took stances and positions on certain topics. I was ignorant of my faith—un-educated.

Over time and through education, deep reflection, prayer, persistence, and grace I was able to overcome, and even embrace, many major concerns as they related to the church. When I began to view the teachings through a spiri-tual instead of a worldly lens, I was much more open to ac-cepting them. I cannot say that I accepted them all without hesitation or question, but I developed a deeper understand-ing of the instructive nature of the tenets. I came to under-stand that the church put teachings in place as guideposts to help us along the path of our faith and to help us navigate through an often morally confusing and tempting world. For example, I learned that part of the church's teaching on artificial birth control had to do with the church's view that marriage is a life-giving union, where couples give freely to one another to create other beautiful lives. By introducing barriers (birth control) to that life-giving relationship, we potentially frustrate God's gift of life through reproduction. Another stumbling block for me was my resistance to con-fessing directly to a priest. I did not understand why I had to tell another human being about my offenses. That seemed humiliating. I wanted to deal with God directly on those matters. Once I came to understand that priests consider this to be one of their most sacred privileges, and once I realized that confession is aimed at healing our souls, I was able to consider the priest as a representative for God and not just another human being. The act of confession became a very healing—though not always easy—tool for spiritual growth.

Even with this increased awareness and some positive momentum, I was sometimes tempted to explore other religions, ones that I perceived as being less restrictive and more open. But then I realized that being a Catholic wasn't necessarily going to be easy, and adopting new ways of thinking would not happen overnight; it would require discipline and persistence, and I definitely would need to commit myself to this journey. Somewhere inside, I knew I was where I needed to be—my roots were in Catholicism. It was how I was raised and from where much of who I am originated. As I accepted this, I was able to see the deeper beauty and meaning in the church teachings, and this helped elevate my spiritual thinking to a new level.

I had started praying on my own and was attending Mass on Sundays again, but I still needed to find someone to talk to about what was happening to me—but in the context of religion and spirituality. A friend at work had been quite involved in the church; he'd attended retreats and tried to stay close to his Catholic faith. One day I invited him to lunch and confided that I really needed to speak to a priest. He gave me the name of a nun he knew—someone he thought might be able to point me in the right direction. When I met with her and told her only a little bit about what had occurred, she seemed neutral, almost apathetic. I didn't get into all of the details but I became quite self-conscious. I'd expected that a nun would have shown more enthusiasm for my awakening, but she appeared unimpressed as

I explained my supernatural happenings. She did suggest, however, that I meet with a local priest, who happened to be at the parish in my neighborhood. She said he was wonderful, very open and accepting. I knew exactly who he was because I had already started to attend Mass at his church.

I contacted the priest and set up an appointment. When we met, I immediately felt at ease and decided to share with him all of the events that had occurred in my life. He was very kind and listened intently. I was uncertain as to what he thought of my story but his main response was that he believed me. He said that God calls us and speaks to us in different ways. I asked him some questions about the Catholic faith, and at the end of our first meeting, he gave me an easy-to-understand book on the catechism, the comprehensive and authoritative source of Catholic teachings. This became absolutely pivotal in helping me to understand the essence of my religion. Over time, I maintained a friendly relationship with this priest—he holds a special place in my heart. In fact, he later shepherded Steve and me through pre-cana counseling sessions required by the church before marriage.

Understanding of and adherence to the church teachings was an essential first step in supporting my spiritual shift but it was only part of the journey. My whole outlook on the world began to change. I had often wondered what it would be like to experience a paradigm shift—and now, here I was, genuinely experiencing one. My whole world was reordered. I became aware of spirituality like never before. I reflected on my behaviors and actions relative to a heavenly world instead of a physical world. My life found a missing dimension—the spiritual dimension of existence—and I realized that I would probably never see things in quite the same way again. I also knew that my life was not in full accordance with how I thought God wanted me to live. I recognized this and accepted that I was at the forefront of a lifelong journey, a continuous evolution of my very person.

Nine

Window to the Soul

During this initial time of exploration, God afforded me a tremendous grace. It lasted for only a brief time but was clearly out of the ordinary. I was given a glimpse into the true essence and experience of the soul while here on earth. Suddenly, I began to interact with the world through the lens of the soul. Things that I had either ignored or never perceived became like amplified assaults upon my innermost being. A simple example is the "news magazine" shows on TV: I regularly watch a particular program on which the hosts engage in antagonistic bantering with guests. Although I had sometimes been annoyed with the aggressive nature of some of the exchanges, the sensationalistic aspect of the format mesmerized me. Then one day, as I watched, I actually began to feel a strange discomfort. It was as if I was experiencing a personal attack from the program's hosts. Their loud voices, aggressive postures, and bullying behavior seemed painfully disrespectful, presumptuous, and judgmental. They lacked all understanding of the impact their behavior had on the people being discussed. It was noticeably devoid of love, peace, understanding, and compassion, and my soul felt wounded by their verbal poundings. How strange this was—I was sitting in my living room, watching the television, yet I understood with certainty the venom that was spreading and the snowballing effect it had on many people. This darkness and violence began to unveil itself in almost all of the programs I attempted to watch, including TV dramas involving cold-case murder mysteries or crime scene investigations. Although I once had been fully engrossed in many of these shows, I simply could not tolerate watching them any longer. I now understood how destructive it was for me to receive entertainment by immersing myself into stories that rely upon someone being viciously tortured or killed, and the forensic analysis of a bloody crime scene. I could no longer understand why anyone would want to write and perpetuate stories that were based on such violent themes. There is enough real pain and suffering in the world. I realized that this type of entertainment is damaging to the soul. To this day, I censor my television and movie watching. I primarily watch only G- and PG-rated movies and regularly shut off programs that conflict with my beliefs.

The same types of experiences carried over to magazines and music. Everywhere I looked there seemed to be abundant anger, accusations, mistrust, gossip, and lack of respect and acceptance for human beings. It is no secret that fashion and entertainment magazines glamorize things like affairs and eating disorders and that we consume these lurid stories with ferocity—I did. Yet having the opportunity to see, albeit briefly, what it does to our spiritual selves—how destructive it is to us personally and ultimately to others in general—made me sad, somewhat overwhelmed, and slightly depressed. I had never recognized the sinister nature of these media vehicles and it was a shock to my system. It was as if I was learning a dark secret about myself that had been veiled and I now had to face that force in my life.

At this time, both my newfound interest in religion and my increased awareness of the world began to create a strong impetus for change within me. I took specific actions to eliminate those things that I understood were damaging and detrimental. I significantly altered the things I read, watched, and listened to. Steve noticed my changes and became worried. I'd stopped wanting to do the things we had been doing together since we started dating—going to movies, going to bars, watching TV programs, and listening to certain music. This caused us to pull away from one another. From his perspective, I had gone to an extreme. Although he understood what precipitated these changes and was very supportive of my spiritual journey, I was becoming a different person from the one he had been dating—and he wasn't sure that he wanted this type of lifestyle. He was keenly aware that he was in a relationship with someone who was becoming a devoted Catholic. This irritated Steve and made him nervous about the future of our relationship. Although he, too, was born and raised Catholic, he saw the oppressive side of the church, the one that insisted that people follow all sorts of strict rules and laws rather than promoting a truly loving, spiritual environment.

One of the big tensions for us was his view on marriage. As I became closer to the church teachings, I was certain that marriage was essential for me and that living together before marriage would no longer be acceptable. When we started dating, I not only thought living together was fine but also that I might never get married. Steve wasn't sure if he ever wanted to get married—he was downright skeptical of it—but he definitely wanted to live together.

For me, despite the risk it posed to our relationship, I knew that I had to follow God's direction and path. I was terrified that it might not include Steve, and I agonized over this for long periods of time. He had spent many years exploring his values and beliefs, and was generally at peace with himself. He was open, accepting, loving, and spiritual, and felt good about where he was in his life. In fact, one day when we were having a philosophical conversation, contemplating how individual actions affect the greater whole of society, he made the comment that he loved all of humanity. I laughed out loud, thinking that he must have been joking. "Did you just say that you love all of humanity?" I asked him.

"Yes," he said. "I do."

I later realized that this was the torch of unconditional love that existed in Steve. It would emerge at various points throughout our journey to help keep both of us strong. On a practical level, this conversation made me realize that he had, indeed, reflected at length about spirituality, which was something I had not yet done.

Steve told me that I couldn't live in a bubble or in isolation and that I had to find a way to function in the world. He continuously reminded me that living to the letter of the law—church law—wasn't the true meaning of being spiritual, and he cautioned me to not get wrapped up in the guidelines, tenets, and laws, lest I miss the experience of living the faith. His observations were good ones, but at that time, I needed to go through this period of withdrawal in order to understand how to reorder my life.

During this time, I prayed very intensely. Whenever possible, I would pray three rosaries a day (this was before Pope John Paul II introduced a fourth rosary), which is the equivalent of approximately 150 individual prayers, mostly Hail Mary's—a form of repetitive prayer, said while holding a chain of connected beads. Each rosary is composed of fifty main beads, which equates to fifty prayers. It is used in a meditative fashion to reflect upon the life of Jesus. This scripturally-based prayer is also known as a popular devotional prayer to Mary. There is some debate about where and when the rosary originated, but it has had a longstanding place in the lives of Catholics throughout history and is a powerful prayer tool. Because the rosary requires focus and discipline, I sometimes would break up my prayers into smaller portions so that I could concentrate better. Other times, I might say one rosary or even all three in one sitting. This was a period of time when I was developing a commitment to prayer. I also continued the practice I had started during Lent of that year, which was attending Mass daily. Sometimes I would go on my lunch break at work. Other times I would attend an evening Portuguese service. Although I don't speak Portuguese, I came to understand the structure and flow of Mass well enough to fully participate, despite the language barrier. One night, the priest at the Portuguese church approached me. Knowing that I wasn't part of the small group of Portuguese parishioners who faithfully attended evening mass, he asked me in his Portuguese accent, "Do you understand?" I immediately said that I did and nodded my head. He just smiled at me. It was not until later that it occurred to me that he might have been asking me if I understood Portuguese. It was at that moment, however, that I realized the great universality of the church. Regardless of where I am in the world, the Catholic services are essentially all the same. The experience is consistent, and I can count on the stability of the rich tradition and heritage of the church. It was very comforting to know that I always have a home at any Catholic Mass, anywhere in the world, regardless of language or nationality.

Along with daily attendance at Mass came an increased desire to go to confession. I started the practice of going to monthly confession. This was an ongoing process of confessing and healing. Each time when I thought I had fully confessed everything, I remembered more things. I suppose that is understandable, as I previously attended only one confession in my entire life and that was out of obligation to make my confirmation—I had an entire childhood and young adulthood to account for! I will never be able to recall every infraction in my life but the joyful relief and energy received from forgiveness is a feeling that will keep bringing me back to the confessional.

Going to confession also led me to the practice of what is called Eucharistic Adoration. This is when the Holy Eucharist (the host), which is what Catholics receive at each Mass, is exposed for adoration and prayer. I went to Adoration events, or Holy Hours, at several churches and eventually learned of a small local chapel that is perpetually open. I periodically drove there and spent time in prayer before the Blessed Sacrament. Sometimes I would be there alone and actually felt scared. It was a strange feeling, almost as if I couldn't handle being alone with Jesus. It may sound odd, but I thought it was almost spooky, and several times I left Adoration to seek comfort with others. Over time, I developed a higher level of comfort just by thinking about being alone with God. I tried to identify the source of my fear. Perhaps it was because of my distance from Him for most of my life. This genuinely bothered me. Eventually, I realized that He was my creator and knows me more completely than any human. I could pretend that being with others would make me feel secure, but He was actually always with me. I concluded that I just needed to get to know Him better and perhaps in a different way. I wanted to get closer to the God of compassion, love, and mercy.

As I continued to grow spiritually, I became involved in a prayer group on Thursday evenings. I learned about the group through one of the church bulletins. One night, not knowing what to expect, I went to my first meeting. It was a fairly small group, about eight to ten people. They started off by saying a joint rosary and then moved on to singing religious songs. Then everyone went into silent meditation. During this time, one could quietly sit with God, meditate, reflect, read the Bible, or even speak in tongues, something I'd never experienced. Many of them had the gift of tongues. Their proclamations were indecipherable to others but it was obvious that they were deeply moved by the Spirit. Several people would very vocally call out, "Praise God!" or "Hallelujah!" These exclamations initially made me uncomfortable, as I had never been in a setting with this type of outward expression of faith. I was used to quiet, private reflection. Over time, I came to appreciate and enjoy the differences of those at the prayer group and learned how much they loved Jesus. I began to look forward to Thursdays as the highlight of my week. It was a fulfilling and enriching experience, and I formed many friendships through the group. In particular, I befriended a man named Scott. He, too, had a very compelling conversion story of how he found God. Through his journey, he had been drawn to a particular devotion known as the Divine Mercy, introduced to the world by a Polish nun named Sister Maria Faustina Kowalska (now Saint Faustina). On February 22, 1931, while in her room at the convent, Saint Faustina saw an image of Jesus appear before her. She wrote that He said to her, "Paint an image according to the pattern you see, with the signature, 'Jesus, I trust in You.'" The image was of Jesus, with one hand covering his heart and the other raised in the sign of a blessing, and two rays flowing from His heart—one red and one white. Jesus told Faustina that He wanted this image to be venerated throughout the world. He promised that the souls that venerate this image would not be lost or perish. Jesus also specifically dictated a special prayer to her known as the "Chaplet of Divine Mercy," said on traditional rosary beads. He told Faustina that through this chaplet, special graces would be granted to those who recite it and souls would obtain everything they asked for, as long as it is consistent with His holy will.[1]

This devotion became another spiritual rock for me. At the same time, it also made me realize that this message from Jesus, given in the early 1900s, was very recent. It is impossible to ignore the fact that so many important messages have been given to us in such recent history. Why so many now? Why at this time in history? Those relating to the Divine Mercy are not separate from those at Medjugorje, nor are they separate from the Gospel in the Holy Bible. They all complement one another and point to God's call for us to return to Him.

Ten

The Flying Picture

In March, I decided to take a trip to Colorado to visit my friend Suzie. This was during the season of Lent leading up to Easter, and I had committed to going to church every day. We went skiing in Vail and found a small chapel there at which to attend Mass. It was intimate and warm, and I had a wonderful feeling about being there. Although I would not have expected it, this Mass proved to be a pivotal moment for me. I listened intently to the readings and then to the priest's homily. He spoke in detail about one of the readings from the Old Testament that tells the story of the Israelites traveling in the desert after they fled from Egypt. The Israelites questioned why God had left them alone in the desert, seemingly abandoned. During his homily, the priest made a multitude of comments that resonated with me, but one statement in particular seemed especially relevant to my current situation. He talked about the significance of the Scripture passage and stated, "God left the Israelites in the desert as a test. He wanted them to know that it was Him—and Him alone—to whom they could turn for solace and relief." That was it! It hit me right then and there. I had been worrying about my relationship with Steve and if we would continue to be together. I wondered if he would leave me because I was going to an extreme with my expression of newfound spirituality. But God spoke directly to me in that moment. He said, "*Amy, I am putting you in your own desert so that you will know that it is me and me alone that will save you.*" That was it. Powerful. Incredible. At that moment, I knew that God's will would be done for Steve and me. Yes, I was scared. Yes, I was uncertain as to what the future might hold. I was terrified that our relationship was close to being over, and I loved him very much. He was everything that I could have wanted in a person and in a life partner, but it was clear that our relationship was up to God. That did not make it easy, but it was clear.

I thought a lot about my relationship with Steve during the trip and talked to Suzie about it. I expressed my fears that he might not want to be on this spiritual journey with me, and the result would be devastating. I really thought I had met someone with whom I could spend my life, but now I was in the middle of this upheaval in my own life and didn't know exactly what was going on. Everything I had known before was changing, so I understood that Steve would not know what to expect from me in the future. He could not possibly know if my evolving spiritual expression would be a life he would want to share with me. Suzie agreed that I was subjecting him to a big test, but she said she could understand my concerns as well as his. That frustrated me; I'd wanted her to say that everything would be fine and that Steve would stick this out with me. But being the friend that she is, she wasn't going to lie and just tell me what she knew I wanted to hear.

When I returned home from Colorado, the relationship question weighed heavily on my mind. On the evening that I got back, Steve and I were sitting on the couch together, watching television. There was tension in the air; both of us had things on our minds that we wanted to share, but neither of us was talking. I started to wonder how I would feel if Steve were to break up with me. I envisioned the scenario in my head—his telling me that it was over; my being devastated, going to church, kneeling in the pews, and crying and praying because I was upset, even though I knew that was what God must have wanted. But just as this disturbing thought ran through my mind, I heard a noise that startled me. There was a scraping sound and a then a thump. I had been resting my head on Steve's shoulder, but when I heard the noise I immediately sat up. I looked over at the radiator cover, where I'd placed a picture of Steve and me, but the picture wasn't there. I stretched over the edge of the couch and saw that it was laying on the carpet, picture-side down. I looked at Steve and asked, "Did what I think just happened actually happen?"

Steve looked at me and nodded.

"Did you see it happen?" I asked.

He nodded again, saying, "It looked as though someone swiped the back of the picture frame and knocked it off the radiator, onto the floor."

I immediately knew that this was a sign for us, a

Framed photo of Steve and me that was knocked over.

calling for us to talk. We shut off the television and shared our feelings about our relationship—that it was strained and that it was a very difficult time for both of us. Steve hit on my worst fear; he said he'd been thinking about dating other people. It broke my heart, but underneath I knew if it was meant to be, it would be. Nonetheless, after a lengthy conversation, we arrived at the best possible conclusion at the time: we both really wanted to make our relationship work. We knew that it would not be easy, but we agreed that we would try to work things out. Steve also disclosed for the first time that the things that happened to me caused him to reevaluate some of his former beliefs on spirituality. With all that I had been going through, I had not even considered that he, too, could be on a new spiritual odyssey.

TAKING
ROOT

"Dear children! Once again I desire to call
you to prayer. When you pray you are much
more beautiful, like flowers, which after the
snow, show all their beauty and all their colors become indescribable. So also you, dear
children, after prayer show before God all
so much more what is beautiful and are be-
loved by Him. Therefore, dear children, pray
and open your inner self to the Lord so that
He makes of you a harmonious and beautiful
flower for Paradise. Thank you for having responded to my call."[1]

~Mary's Message of December 18, 1986~

Eleven

Life Is a Prayer

*After my trip to Colorado, my interest in visiting Med-*jugorje increased. I hoped for a richer, deeper understanding of the messages and a clearer understanding of my life's true direction. Steve and I had briefly discussed the possibility of going there together, but now we were ready to secure a spot with a tour group.

Steve and I asked our parents if they wanted to take the trip with us. Everyone agreed that a pilgrimage to Medjugorje was a once-in-a-lifetime opportunity. I called a woman named Rena, who not only was a tour guide but also happened to be the woman who had been translating for the visionary, Ivanka, when my mother saw her speak at St. Joseph's Church in Maine. Her voice when she greeted me on the phone was soft and gentle. I immediately sensed that she was the right person to travel with, and after later receiving more detailed information on the pilgrimage by mail, we all decided that we wanted Rena as our guide. Within a few days, we were booked for an April pilgrimage to Medjugorje.

About a week after we secured our reservations, my mother called Rena to ask her advice about clothes and other items to bring on the trip. She also asked her the name of the hotel where we'd be staying—and she almost fainted when she heard the answer. As it turned out, we wouldn't be going to a hotel, instead we were staying at Ivanka's house—one of the six visionaries!

I practically jumped into the air when my mother passed along this news—it was absolutely amazing! Since 1981 more than 20 million pilgrims had journeyed to Medjugorje[1] to catch a glimpse of the visionaries, to hear them speak about their experiences, and to get close to them. Now, we actually would be staying in the home of one of them.

Less than a year after the words "Medjugorje, spiritual awakening" first came to me, I was on my way to a tiny village in a former Communist country to visit with a woman who receives visions of the Virgin Mary and messages from heaven. If I had any doubt about my involvement in Medjugorje, this helped confirm that I was, indeed, on the right path.

At the time of our pilgrimage, Bosnia-Herzegovina and Croatia were still on the US government travel watchlist and were not recommended as places to visit. Although the Bosnian war had officially ended in 1995, the region was still considered unstable and dangerous for travelers. My father initially had expressed reservations about making the trip abroad, but the potentially dangerous circumstances never concerned me. I knew this trip was part of my destiny and I was going to go.

April finally arrived, and we traveled by plane and then by bus with Rena and four other wonderful people who joined the pilgrimage. Rena was originally from Croatia and had a detailed understanding of the conflict that led to the Bosnian war and other regional conflicts. Her knowledge of history, her native familiarity, and her deep, certain faith in Jesus led to a remarkable and impressionable experience for all of us. She not only guided us physically on our pilgrimage but also set the spiritual tone. She kept us focused on praying at every opportunity. Wherever we went, whether on a bus or eating dinner, we prayed, prayed, and prayed. We said rosaries, attended Mass at least twice each day, and said prayers before every meal. We sometimes felt like we were in spiritual boot camp. There were things we knew, like the flow of the Mass, and new things we learned, like songs and prayers. For me, this spiritual regimen was fine, given the devotion I had recently experienced. Yet for all of us, including Steve's family and mine, it didn't take long to distinguish between the hard but fruitful work of a pilgrimage and the leisurely recreation of a vacation.

We arrived at Ivanka's home by late afternoon and discovered that the Italian group of pilgrims who were supposed to share our accommodations had canceled their trip. I was thrilled that we had Ivanka all to ourselves! She was a kind and gracious hostess. She cooked and served us food in abundance, and the meals were delicious and satisfying. We all felt somewhat odd that she was waiting on us and catering to our needs. After all, this was a woman who, for the past twenty years, had regular interactions with the Virgin Mary. She received messages for herself, the parish of Medjugorje, and for the world. We felt as though we should have been waiting on her.

One night after dinner, Ivanka sat down with us at the long table in her basement that must have held many pilgrims over the years. She sat in a chair and, through Rena's translation assistance, invited us to ask her questions. We were quite interested in how Ivanka was able to manage her busy life, hosting pilgrims and taking care of three children, a husband, and a home, all while living out the messages from Mary. We asked how she had time to pray and what her prayer life was like. She told us that she tried to set aside time in the morning for prayer before her day began. Then she told us something very important, something that changed us all. She said, "Whatever you do with love is a prayer." Whether it is cooking, cleaning, or working in an office, if it is done with love, it is a prayer. In fact, she said, "Life is a prayer."

With all of the supernatural events that had happened in my life and with the special interventions that preceded this trip, I was not sure what more I could have possibly obtained from my trip to Medjugorje. I had known it would be special, but the awakening I experienced was already special. Staying at Ivanka's house, however, yielded a gift that wasn't *out* of this world but one that was *for* this world. The biggest lesson I took away from this very special woman was that just being who we are—in our everyday life and chosen vocation, whatever it may be—is a way to unite ourselves with God and to serve Him. In other words, God calls us to love and be peaceful, kind, and merciful in

Ivanka and me outside of her home.

whatever type of life we have. We don't need to be priests, nuns, or even visionaries. We just need to live our life as a prayer and take every moment as an opportunity to show God's love to others.

Twelve

Living the Messages in Medjugorje

In her communications to the visionaries and ultimately to the world, Mary has repeatedly shared five main messages. Although I initially discovered these in the book *Medjugorje, The Message* and learned about them through other research, my actually being in Medjugorje made them come alive for me in an entirely different way.

The first message Mary gives is peace. When she first appeared to the visionaries, she was reported to have said very early on, "Peace, peace, peace—and only peace. Peace must rule between man and God and also among the people."[1] She also called herself by the name Queen of Peace, and is known in Medjugorje and around the world by this name.[2] Mary's message of peace is the overarching principle for all the other messages, and it is universal; peace is applicable to every human being on this earth. It is most important, however, to recognize that mankind needs God to achieve this state of peace. In fact, Jesus himself has said this in visions to Saint Faustina. On page 132 of her diary, she wrote that Jesus said, "Humanity will not find peace until it turns trustfully to Divine Mercy."[3] Mary is saying the same thing. We need to have peace with God and then peace with one another. Thus, in the overall plan, Mary shares ways in which to get closer to God in order to obtain that peace. Prayer is an essential and critical element in this plan. One of her messages conveys the power of prayer. "Dear children! Today I wish to call you to pray, pray, pray! In prayer you shall perceive the greatest joy and the way out of every situation that has no exit."[4]

In Medjugorje, we were able to experience firsthand how the messages that Mary has communicated to the visionaries over the years manifest themselves, especially relating to prayer. There, we not only participated in formal prayer, such as Mass and public rosaries, but we also hiked up Podbrdo (Apparition Hill), where Mary first appeared to the six children. It is a relatively small hill that features a series of stone images depicting the story of Jesus' life. The reliefs are scattered along a path leading up the hillside. About halfway up the hill is the exact spot where Mary first appeared to the children. A basic but impressive cross overlooks the village from the hill.

Many people struggle up the rocky terrain, slowly making their way to the top for prayer and reflection. We made the same trek as millions of other pilgrims and experienced the depth, mystery, and inspiration that others have surely known. There is something special about standing on the very ground where Mary first appeared to the vi-

The cross on Apparition Hill where Mary first appeared.

sionaries in 1981. It is there, on that hill, that she said that a permanent sign would be left for mankind that will serve to validate the authenticity of her apparitions.[5] Steve's mother, Betty, was not able to climb up with us due to a hip injury and instead stayed behind and looked through the gift shops. During that time, she bought me a beautiful rosary that has its beads made from Podbrdo's rocks, and features a medallion that contains soil from the hill enclosed within a small capsule. Every time I pray with that rosary it transports me back there, and I lose myself in its mystery all over again.

Rosary given to me by Steve's mother, Betty.

We also hiked up Mt. Krizevac (Cross Mountain) where, in 1934, the parishioners of Medjugorje completed their construction of a giant concrete cross at the mountain's peak to mark the nineteen hundredth anniversary of the Crucifixion. Many hikers pray on their mile-high journey up the mountain.

John, one of our fellow pilgrims, inspired some of us to climb the mountain in our bare feet, as a form of penance. He took off his sneakers and socks. Then Steve's father took his off, and then Steve and I followed suit. Part of me wanted to do this because Steve's father was doing it. He had diabetes, which can cause significant pain in one's feet. If he was willing to walk barefoot up the mountain, I thought that I—a healthy thirty-something—should be able to do it. I did not totally comprehend the value of walking barefoot as a penance, but I did understand that it was a form of reparation for my wrongdoings. I climbed very slowly, walking over sharp rocks and jutting stones. I didn't mind the discomfort, however, as I was focused on my meditation at the Stations of the Cross along the ascending pathway and on Jesus' passion.

As we approached each station, we reflected briefly in silence and then sang a moving hymn that includes the words, "Were you there when they crucified my Lord?" As we paused, prayed, and sang, I still did not really understand the point of intentionally experiencing physical pain or discomfort for God. Yet somehow, I knew there was merit in it, and I embraced it for what is was. Hiking the mountain barefoot was one of the most fulfilling experiences of my life. In a small way, I was able to offer something to God. Even if it was just a barefoot hike up a mountain, it symbolized my willingness to accept some of the spiritual acts and practices that would ultimately lead to positive outcomes for me along my life journey.

As we hiked up the mountains and visited different areas near the village, some carried sealed envelopes with them that contained the intentions and prayers from relatives and friends back home. Some were instructed to leave the envelopes at the base of the cross at the top of Mt. Krizevac or in St. James Church. Other envelopes provided specific requests for which we were asked to pray. Whatever they were, we carried them with us, physically and spiritually, and fulfilled their wishes. Wherever we traveled and whatever we did, our activities were immersed in prayer, and our thoughts were with those at home. I thought a great deal about my sister, Kelli. The night before we departed for our trip, I had received a call from her. She had something to tell me that no one else knew except my mother—she was fairly certain that she was pregnant. She wasn't married, but she had recently become engaged. She asked me to pray for her on the trip. I assured her that I would pray for both her and the baby.

At the church in Medjugorje, Mass is held for pilgrims throughout the day in a number of different languages. We attended one English Mass in the early morning and then an evening celebration and Mass, which lasted three hours. We arrived at the church an hour early to secure our seats. As we expected, it was standing room only. This was the first time in my life that I had seen a church overflowing and the first time I ever arrived an hour early. I knew this was something very special. The evening celebration started out with the joyful and sorrowful rosaries. The entire assembly participated in this, and their faith was easily evident. Then at precisely 5:40 (6:40 in summer), during the rosary, Mary arrived at the church, unseen except to the visionaries, who no longer appear publicly in the church. Everyone paused, recognized her unseen arrival, and then resumed praying of the rosary. It is said through the visionaries that Mary gives a special blessing to all those present and also gives her motherly blessing over all religious articles people bring with them. I accepted this on faith, and at the time she was said to arrive, I asked her silently to bless the religious articles I had purchased.

After the pause and at the conclusion of the second rosary, the Mass began. The Mass is celebrated in a very holy and reverent manner. It is never rushed or hurried. Music is always fully integrated into the service, and the large screen in the front of the church displays words to the music, encouraging participation by the attendees. I enjoyed the camaraderie of my fellow churchgoers as we sang loudly and passionately during the Mass.

The Gospel is read in a number of languages to accommodate pilgrims from different countries. Everyone remains standing until they hear the Gospel in their native tongue. Sometimes people remain standing until the last Gospel translation is shared. During the Mass, people concentrate on the celebration and the mystery of what is occurring. Even though the homily (a talk based on the day's biblical passages) is said in Croatian, attendees participate in their own private way. Perhaps part of our inspiration and awe was seeing the sheer number of priests on the altar celebrating Mass at the same time. On any given day, it is not uncommon to see more than twenty priests sharing the altar in celebration of the Eucharist. Currently across America, parishes are closing and consolidating due to the lack of available priests. Seeing all of those priests on the altar in Medjugorje was inspirational; it was like participating in a revival.

After Mass, the assembly remains in the church to say additional prayers and rosaries. On different nights during the week other types of worship activities begin after the evening celebration. On some nights, there is Veneration of the Cross or Eucharistic Adoration. More singing, praying, and healing goes on until 10:30 or 11:00 each night.

When I think back on these different events, I become as tired as I was on the trip. We literally spent our entire time thinking about Jesus, and praying, and participating in services and spiritual exercises. I had never prayed so much in my entire life.

The most amazing part of this, however, was not the pilgrims who journey to Medjugorje; rather, it was the local people in the village who participated in these services

Saint James Church.

Statue of Mary in the front courtyard at St. James Church.

regularly. Some people attend the evening celebration every night. They demonstrate such great perseverance and endurance; their ongoing faith is inspiring. They are true witnesses to God's love and light and are the true examples of strength that many of us needed throughout our journey in Medjugorje and our journey toward God. They typify what Mary says in a third message—one of having and keeping faith. Faith means believing fully in God, believing that He is with us and sustains us. Faith is having trust in God and putting that trust into action.

I think our families would agree that the fourth message—fasting—was the part of the trip we all dreaded. The messages from Mary call people to return to the Old Testament practice of fasting. In particular, Mary recommends that people fast on both Wednesdays and Fridays on bread and water alone. She indicates that this practice will help us to grow spiritually and will help us to detach ourselves from earthly goods.

The first night we spent at Ivanka's house was a Wednesday night. We had endured a very long trip from the United States to Germany, through Croatia, and then up the coastline into the mountains of Bosnia-Herzegovina. We were tired and hungry, but we expected that we would be required to observe a fast. After we met Ivanka, we sat at the very long table in her basement, and Ivanka served us soup and bread. We quickly finished our servings and looked at one another, wondering how much soup was left and who was going to take it. My father spoke up saying that he would like the rest of the soup if no one else wanted it. I think we all wanted it, but everyone graciously said that he could finish it. We expected that this was our full meal, so we sure were happy when Ivanka walked through the door with a large plate of fish! Then, Ivanka came out again and again with plate after plate of food. Rena explained that this, too, was a type of fast because we were not eating red meat or poultry and were eating *simple* foods.

We talked for a while about fasting, and Rena shared something very important: we are all called in a unique way to respond to Mary's messages, and we must do what we are capable of doing. She explained that some people who cannot fast on bread and water alone choose other fasts, such as giving up sweets. Fasting does not have to be giving up certain foods. A fast can be giving up anything that could be construed as difficult to give up—a sacrifice—such as not watching TV or refraining from talking negatively or gossiping about people. Although Mary's message remains unchanged and is ideal, we did learn that there are indeed other ways to fast that also represent spiritual cleansing or purification—it doesn't have to be eating just bread and water. During the rest of the pilgrimage, we did fast on Wednesday and Friday. When I returned home, I took up fasting and tried to be literal to Mary's request. On most Wednesdays for a long while, I ate only bread and drank water and coffee. On Fridays, I gave up eating meat.

Mary's fifth message is about conversion. When I first heard the word conversion, I wasn't quite sure what it meant. After reading and exploring the topic, I learned that conversion means ordering one's life and one's actions toward God. I also learned that conversion is not a discrete action. In fact, conversion happens on a daily basis. After all, we are all weak and fall down, and there is never a day when we don't need God's grace and assistance.

One of the ways that conversion is supported at Medjugorje is through the practice of confession. Like so many other things that seemed to fall into place, going to confession there was a lot easier than trying to get to confession at home. At St. James Church, there was a long row of confessionals, and priests heard confessions throughout the day in as many languages as one could imagine. (At home, however, confession might be offered only once a week for an hour or by appointment in many churches.) I once heard someone say that the truth always comes out in Medjugorje. Certainly, going to confession there helped me. Although I had already started that practice, certain things that I had forgotten now bothered me, and I had the opportunity to clear my conscience. Many people are uncomfortable with the practice of confession. They believe that it is not appropriate because God does not expect us to confess to another human rather than directly to God. According to scripture, however, God imparted a special power of forgiveness and reconciliation that Catholics believe resides with the priests. This is exemplified in the scripture passage of John 20:23, "Whose sins you forgive are forgiven them, and whose sins you retain are retained."[6] Confession is not easy, nor is it supposed to be, but I do know that the weight that's lifted off of my shoulders after a good confession is a joy that is indescribable. And it's a joy that's only understood by those who truly believe that it is Jesus, in the confessional, forgiving sins and helping us to start anew. It is very interesting that most priests say that hearing confessions is one of the most special gifts given to them by Jesus. In fact, they often see it as an honor and one of the most important aspects of their vocation. I am not a theologian or a student of the church. I can only say that I sincerely believe that most priests carry out this obligation with the utmost respect and devotion.

In addition to the main messages of Medjugorje, which are compelling in and of themselves, there is something still more mysterious that intrigues many about Mary's visits to earth—the secrets that Mary has and will impart to all six visionaries. To date, some of the visionaries have received all of the secrets, but some have not.[7] It is believed that when all the visionaries receive all ten secrets, the apparitions will cease, and the secrets will begin to unfold. Some of the secrets pertain only to the visionaries, to the local parish in Medjugorje, and to the Catholic Church. Others, however, apply to the entire world. It is believed that some secrets are grave and a chastisement for the sins of the world. What we do know is that the visionaries continuously stress the urgency of the messages and encourage us to convert our hearts—and to convert now.

As we learned, Mary will leave a permanent sign at the site of her first apparition on Podbrdo (Apparition Hill), and this permanent sign will be indestructible. It is also said that this sign will serve as an impetus for many more people to convert to God. Before this sign is left, however, a warning will be given to the world.

In the early days of the apparitions, the following is part of a letter written by a local priest to the Pope regarding these events:

"After the apparition of the Blessed Virgin on November 30, 1983, Maria Pavlovic came to me and said, 'The Madonna says that the Supreme Pontiff and the Bishop must be advised immediately of the urgency and great importance of the message of Medjugorje.'

This letter seeks to fulfill that duty.

1. Five young people (Vicka Ivankovic, Maria Pavlovic, Ivanka Ivankovic, Ivan Dragicevic, and Jakov Colo) see an apparition of the Blessed Virgin every day. The experience in which they see her is a fact that can be checked by direct observation. It has been filmed. During the apparitions, the youngsters do not react to light, they do not hear sounds, they do not react if someone touches them, they feel that they are beyond time and space. All of the youngsters basically agree that:

- "We see the Blessed Virgin just as we see anyone else. We pray with her, we speak to her, and we can touch her."
- "The Blessed Virgin says that world peace is at a critical stage. She repeatedly calls for reconciliation and conversion."
- "She has promised to leave a visible sign for all humanity at the site of the apparitions of Medjugorje."
- "The period preceding this visible sign is a time of grace for conversion and deepening the faith."

- "The Blessed Virgin has promised to disclose ten secrets to us. So far, Vicka Ivankovic has received eight. Marija Pavlovic received the eighth one on December 8, 1983. Jakov Colo, Ivan Dragicevic and Ivanka Ivankovic have each received nine. Only Mirjana Dragicevic has received all ten."
- "These apparitions are the last apparitions of the Blessed Virgin on earth. That is why they are lasting so long and occurring so frequently."

2. The Blessed Virgin no longer appears to Mirjana Dragicevic. The last time she saw one of the daily apparitions was Christmas 1982. Since then the apparitions have ceased for her, except on her birthday (March 18, 1983). Mirjana knew that this would occur.

According to Mirjana, the Madonna confided the tenth and last secret to her during the apparition on December 25, 1982. She also disclosed the dates on which the different secrets will come to pass. The Blessed Virgin has revealed to Mirjana many things about the future, more than to any of the other youngsters so far. For that reason I am reporting below what Mirjana told me during our conversation on November 5, 1983. I am summarizing the substance of her account, without word-for-word quotations:

- Mirjana said that before the visible sign is given to humanity, there will be three warnings to the world. The warnings will be in the form of events on earth. Mirjana will be a witness to them. Three days before one of the admonitions, Mirjana will notify a priest of her choice. The witness of Mirjana will be a confirmation of the apparitions and a stimulus for the conversion of the world.

- After the admonitions, the visible sign will appear on the site of the apparitions in Medjugorje for all the world to see. The sign will be given as a testimony to the apparitions and in order to call the people back to the faith.

- The ninth and tenth secrets are serious. They concern chasticement for the sins of the world. Punishment is inevitable, for we cannot expect the whole world to be converted. The punishment can be diminished by prayer and penance, but it cannot be eliminated. Mirjana says that one of the evils that threatened the world, the one contained in the seventh secret, has been averted, thanks to prayer and fasting. That is why the Blessed Virgin continues to encourage prayer and fasting: *"You have forgotten that through prayer and fasting you can avert war and suspend the laws of nature."*

- After the first admonition, the others will follow in a rather short time. Thus, people will have some time for conversion.
- That interval will be a period of grace and conversion. After the visible sign appears, those who are still alive will have little time for conversion. For that reason, the Blessed Virgin invites us to urgent conversion and reconciliation.
- The invitation to prayer and penance is meant to avert evil and war, but most of all to save souls.
- According to Mirjana, the events predicted by the Blessed Virgin are near. By virtue of this experience, Mirjana proclaims to the world: 'Hurry, be converted; open your hearts to God.'"[8]

The visionaries have said that the secrets will unfold in their lifetimes and that life in the world we know will change. In August 1983, in an interview, Father Tomislav Vlasic said that after the secrets are revealed "men [mankind] will believe like in ancient times. What will change and how it will change we will not know until the secrets are revealed."[9]

We are encouraged not to focus on the secrets, yet in all us of lies an insatiable desire to know what these secrets are. Mary's direction has been straightforward and constant regarding how to handle what some people suspect are cataclysmic events for the world: return to God through peace, prayer, conversion, faith, and fasting. For those who do this, there need be no concern.

Thirteen

Disciples of All Nations

*While in Medjugorje and during our travels, we were fortu-*nate to be able to go on several day trips to surrounding areas. One day we traveled to Mostar, a large war-torn city in Bosnia-Herzegovina. Many of the buildings were dilapidated and riddled with bullet and other holes caused by bombs or grenades. We went to see the iconic bridge that allows passage between the two sides of the city. The bridge was destroyed during the war and, at the time of our visit, was being repaired. I remembered seeing a news piece about the bridge on a popular TV program. The report highlighted how the constant state of disrepair of the bridge symbolized the lingering effects and fallout of the war. The devastation from the war was clearly evident. Armed Italian military patrolling the fragile area was a strong reminder of the underlying conflict that still persists among people in that area.

While in Mostar, we also had the chance to visit the city's largest Catholic church, Saint Peter and Paul, which had been damaged severely in the war. We entered the church grounds and walked around the garden area. There had been a wedding, and the bridal party was taking pictures. We noticed that the groom's face was disfigured. He was a handsome young man who probably had been injured during the war. As we continued to walk around, we were greeted by a friendly priest. He introduced himself as Father Tomislav Pervan. Rena had arranged for us to meet him. To our amazement and delight, he informed us that he had actually been one of the Medjugorje parish priests during the early years of the apparitions. How fortunate and touched we all felt; Mary was continuing to guide us on our journey, helping us to feel close to miracles at every moment. Father Pervan continued to talk with us and then offered most graciously to give us a private tour of the church. It had been burned down during the war, and when it was rebuilt, was made entirely of concrete so that it could never again be so totally destroyed. It has a huge underground chapel that accommodates a large number of people so that Mass and any other activities can proceed uninterrupted if the main floor is ever deemed unsafe. We noticed a large wooden statue of the Virgin Mary holding Jesus in the underground chapel. Father Pervan told us that it was found beneath the rubble of the burned church. Miraculously, it had not burned and was restored for display.

On the trip back to Ivanka's, soldiers stopped our bus as we tried to leave the city. Our guide exited the bus and answered questions about himself and his tour group. We were all anxious and nervous and felt vulnerable in a

Saint Peter and Paul Church in Mostar, nearly reconstructed.

Restored statue found beneath rubble of the burned church.

Father Tomislav Pervan giving our group a tour of St. Peter and Paul Church. Steve's father (far left), me (3rd from left), my father (4th from left), Fr. Pervan (center), and Steve (3rd from right.)

foreign country that still was in strife. I had flashes of ending up in a foreign jail and being detained indefinitely. Fortunately, within a few minutes, we were permitted to proceed on our journey. We all sighed with relief—unharmed but shaken up a bit.

On another day, we took a trip to a small chapel not far from Medjugorje. This chapel had recently acquired an image of Jesus, a painted replica of the one shown to Saint Faustina and associated with the Divine Mercy devotion. It was reported that a special healing had been associated with this particular image in this chapel. We didn't have all of the details but were excited to see the small, quaint chapel as we diversified our travel during the pilgrimage. We arrived at the chapel during the hour of Divine Mercy (sometime after 3:00 in the afternoon) and began to pray together as a group. We were the only people there. It was simple and intimate. We stayed no more than a half hour but the small chapel, by a river in a remote valley, away from the bustle of the major pilgrimage site, presented us with a nice opportunity to reflect on the wonderful pilgrimage God had afforded all of us. When we returned to Medjugorje, we met a woman who also had visited the chapel. She gave several of us copies of the Divine Mercy image. Ten years later, I still have that image framed and visible in my home.

As the pilgrimage came to a close, we prepared ourselves for the return trip home. Before we left, however, we had one more stop to make. Rena had asked us earlier if we would like to make a financial contribution to a refugee camp. She said that the money would be used to purchase food for them and that we would personally deliver the food on our way out of Medjugorje. Rena said that sometimes people did not want to go there because it put a damper on their pilgrimage. We did not share that sentiment. In fact, if we had learned anything from our trip, we learned that this is what Jesus would want of us.

When we arrived at the refugee camp, I caught sight of a gaunt man in baggy clothes. He was walking slowly toward the bus as it pulled in, and he had a broad grin on his face. I struggled with this contradiction—he clearly was suffering, yet he was smiling. And then I understood: he was hungry, and we were bringing food. Before we arrived, Rena had explained the dire situation in which the refugees were living. The government provided only one meal a day—a bowl of soup at lunchtime. It was next to impossible for them to secure employment, except for a few who sometimes managed to get odd jobs in the community, so most were sus-

Framed Divine Mercy image on display in our home.

tained by the type of support that Rena coordinated. Rena further explained that the camp was like a trap. During the war, these residents were forced out of their homes and communities and fled with only the clothes on their back. Their identification papers and any other identifying documents were stolen or lost. Without any papers to prove their identity or citizenship, they were literally stuck in this camp, perhaps forever trapped in this horror.

The bus doors opened, and we exited to meet a group of refugees who quickly gathered around. Standing side by side with these suffering people was difficult. We really did not know what to say or do. A small glimmer of hope seemed to cross their faces as they anticipated eating whatever food we brought. We looked around the camp briefly and tried to communicate with those who spoke English. I was shown inside one of the tents, where a family of four lived. It was nothing more than a shack. Inside was one makeshift bed where the entire family slept. There were clothes littered about the bed, probably used to keep them warm at night. Other than that, there appeared to be next to nothing. The small living space was defined only by ropes with hanging blankets serving as walls, providing a modicum of privacy. As I struggled to comprehend how an entire family of four could exist in these conditions, an intense sadness overwhelmed me. I interacted briefly with the young family—the parents and their two young daughters. The smallest child was wearing an oversized jean dress that fell off of her shoulders and brushed against the ground. There was a vacant look in all of their eyes, as if their souls had been taken from them. I later learned that the smallest child was born there. It is hard to imagine the physical and emotional suffering of living in and being born in a refugee camp—some of the most painful circumstances for people in our world.

We did not stay long. Rena had, at one time, lived in a refugee camp herself, and she preferred not to stay for long periods of time. Before we boarded the bus, the group of refugees crowded around, and someone led several prayers. This was a deeply humbling experience. I witnessed a true expression of faith. With all that these people had to complain about, they still took the time to give praise to God for His goodness. I will never forget our visit or that man who walked toward us, smiling, as we arrived. That image and what the man represents will be forever etched in my mind.

Rena gave every group who traveled with her a unique and special name. After prayerful thought, she called us the Disciples of All Nations. There were eleven of us on this trip, just as there were eleven disciples who went to the mountain in Galilee to see Jesus after his resurrection. When Jesus appeared to the disciples, He instructed them, "Go, therefore, and make disciples of all nations, baptizing them in the name of the Father, and of the Son, and of the Holy Spirit, teaching them to observe all that I have commanded you" (Matthew 28:19–20).[1] Although we had not yet fully assimilated all that we had learned on our pilgrimage, we knew one thing for certain: we were forever changed by this journey and now had a new responsibility of living out what we had learned.

Our MIR Peace pilgrimage group, that Rena named the Disciples of All Nations, on the steps of St. James Church. Back row: Steve's father, Eugene. Middle row: my father. Front row: my mother (2ⁿᵈ from left), me (holding sign), Steve (to my right), Steve's mother, Betty (far right.)

Fourteen

The American Embassy

Once we left the camp, we headed back down the mountain and past the Adriatic Sea. We spent one night at a hotel in Croatia and then rose early in the morning to complete the second part of the journey, which took us back to the airport in Split. From Split, we flew to Germany, where we would get a flight back to the United States. In Germany, as we prepared to board the plane for the final leg of the trip, Steve's mother, Betty, realized she did not have her passport with her. Apparently, she had packed it in her suitcase that had already been loaded onto the plane. She and her husband, Gene, got into a long debate about where the passport should have been packed, where they thought it was, and who was responsible for the mishap. In the end, they were not able to board the plane with us and were told that they had to go to the US Embassy in Germany to straighten out the situation. This was only about nine months after the September 11 terrorist attacks, so we were not optimistic that they would get back to the States quickly.

After they left the airport, the rest of us decided to begin a rosary for them and asked for the Blessed Mother's intervention to ensure that they made it home safely and swiftly. In the meantime, Betty and Gene got a cab at the embassy and began the laborious process of trying to get approval to return to the States. They soon discovered, however, that there was another unforeseen problem. Although Betty had been living in the United States for almost forty years, she was technically a British citizen who had a British passport, not an American one. The embassy representatives advised Steve's parents that it was going to be a very long wait. In fact, they were told that they would not be able to fly home that same day. After almost nine hours of waiting, Betty finally got what she needed. They walked out of the embassy to find their original cab driver still waiting for them. He had stayed there the entire time and was ready to return them to the airport. They gave the cab driver every last bit of money they had—over three hundred dollars—and thanked him profusely. It was nothing short of a miracle that he had waited the entire time for them. When they returned to the airport, they were pleasantly surprised to learn that Steve had already booked two seats for them on the next available flight back to New York. Everything fell into place.

On our own earlier flight back to the States, the rest of us felt exhausted from the trip but at the same time were exhilarated. I started to watch an in-flight movie, but before long, I dozed off and soon was dreaming. In this dream, I was given my "final grace" of the trip to Medjugorje. In the dream, I recalled two situations that occurred during Steve's and my courtship, which I had forgotten about. They both had to do with me pretending to others that I was single during the time that we were dating—once on a trip to Colorado and once on a trip to Aruba with my friend. Although it was nothing serious, I did feel that I had betrayed him in some way, and it bothered me deeply. I realized that I had not been fully honest in each of those circumstances and that was disrespectful to him and our relationship. As I woke up from my dream, I heard dialogue in the movie where the wife says to her husband, "It's not about the awakening of the head but the awakening of the heart." Indeed, my heart had been awakened! I had the opportunity to tell Steve about these situations that had been recalled, thankfully, into my consciousness. I was scared to talk to Steve about what I had dreamed, but I mustered up the courage to share what had come to me. When I finished talking, Steve looked at me and smiled gently. "Thanks, hon," he said. He appreciated my sharing this with him, he said, but insisted that my concerns were not that big of a deal. But for me, they were. I did not want to have anything clouding my conscience; I did not want to have any untruths left between us. Now the slate was clean—no secrets, no lies, and no tiny fabrications. It was after this exchange that I felt that the door opened wide for the possibility of a future together. I knew I loved Steve, and now I knew in my heart that there was nothing stopping us from going forward together in this life as a couple.

On November 9, 2002, roughly six months after returning from Medjugorje, Steve and I were married in a

My sister, Michele, prepares Steve & me for our walk down the aisle as newlyweds.

beautiful Catholic church, Saints Peter and Paul, in Lewiston, Maine. It's the very same church where my parents had been married almost forty-five years earlier—and coincidentally, bears the same name as the church we visited in Mostar. Our married life together began on that day, and our spiritual life together also commenced in a new and exciting way—a way that neither of us quite envisioned.

BLOSSOMING

"Dear children! May this time be a time of personal prayer for you, so that the seed of faith may grow in your hearts; and may it grow into a joyful witness to others. I am with you and I desire to inspire you all: grow and rejoice in the Lord who has created you. Thank you for having responded to my call."[1]

~Mary's Message of January 25, 2010~

Fifteen

My First Novena

After returning from Medjugorje and getting married, I continued my spiritual journey and began to truly awaken my heart to the needs of others. After spending almost a year learning about Medjugorje, delving into my religion, and contemplating God, I believed that I had to outwardly manifest this spiritual awakening. Although I continued to go to Mass, read the Bible, pray, and work on my personal growth, I felt a growing desire to do more for others and, specifically, to pray more for others. I had been given much and had so many graces that I knew I needed to use my gifts to benefit others. The prayers I said for others often were directed to saints. I prayed novenas, or nine-day prayers, for specific intentions. I prayed for souls who had passed on from this world—family members, friends, and everyone I had known. Praying for others was something between

God and me and was a way for me to demonstrate my faith. When I prayed for others, it was out of love for God, because this is what He asks of us—to care for and support one another through love.

One of the things I learned from a fellow pilgrim on my trip to Medjugorje was to always pray for a specific person or a specific intention to ensure that prayers are as fruitful as possible. So that is what I did. I also continued to pray for myself for guidance, direction, and strength.

As I mentioned, I first prayed to saints, particularly those who send a sign to the person who prays. I prayed to Saint Therese, a saint who often sends roses as a sign that prayers are heard. The Society of the Little Flower website displays her famous quote: "After my death, I will let fall a shower of roses. I will spend my heaven doing good upon earth. I will raise up a mighty host of little saints. My mission is to make God loved." The first time I prayed to her was for a family friend. The friend was experiencing a particularly difficult time with his father-in-law, and a rift that existed between the two was growing greater, threatening to permanently damage the family bonds. I prayed intently for healing and reconciliation between my friend and his father-in-law. I prayed that they would find a way to reconcile and find peace with one another. I prayed for nine days and ended my novena on All Saints Day, a day of recognition of the remarkable saints of the church. I poured my heart and trust into these prayers and believed that Saint Therese would intervene before God in this very difficult family situation. I was grateful for the coincidence that the prayer culminated on a day when people all over the world were thanking God for the saints. I thought this might make the novena even more powerful. A few days after completing the novena prayer, Steve and I were walking to a restaurant. It was a November day and slightly cool. Most of the trees had dropped their leaves, and the flowers had long since died for the season. As we passed a particular area, something told me to stop and turn around, and there before me was a rose bush in full bloom! I excitedly pointed this out to Steve—I had just received a sign from Saint Therese. We marveled at the directness of the sign of roses.

Internally, I continued to keep a silent vigil for our friends. Within a few months, Steve heard from the friend for whom I had been praying, and Steve shared some remarkable news. He became inspired to write and deliver a letter to his father-in-law in an attempt to make peace with him. He then had a discussion with him, after which he told us that they were now on the path to reconciling their differences. I was absolutely elated! Although my prayers may not have been the sole reason for this reunion, I was certain—based on the sign from Saint Therese—that my prayers had somehow contributed to a positive outcome. This friend had visited my apartment almost a year earlier, during the time when the unusual things were happening to me. He teased me at the time, saying that I was scared of ghosts. I thought it was ironic that a year later, I had the pleasure of witnessing his spiritual effort, something to which I secretly felt linked. I've never told him about my part in this story, but I'm sure he would attest that his actions had a positive impact on his family. In my opinion, it is proof of the power of prayer.

Sixteen

Apartments

*Once I realized how powerful Saint Therese was, I con-*tinued to pray to her. In 2004, I prayed for my sister Kelli's needs. As a single mother with two children, she had her share of difficulties and she was now having a hard time finding an apartment.

I'd completed the novena for Kelli a week or so earlier and had decided to travel to Maine to visit my family. At a rest stop along the way, I carried my daughter Madeline, who was only about six months old, into the lobby of a restaurant. Behind us, a woman entered the restaurant and smiled. She pointed to Madeline saying, "What a lovely little shirt. Look at those cute roses." I smiled back at the woman but was slightly perplexed by her comment. I looked at Madeline's shirt and for the first time noticed that the print was actually roses. I had put the shirt on her many

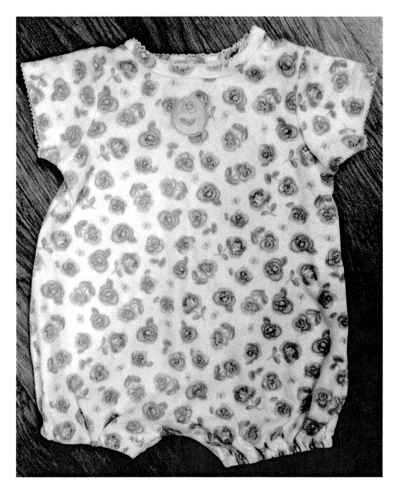

Maddy's rose-covered baby outfit.

times before, but I had never realized the swirled red-and-white design was roses. I left the restaurant, still thinking how unusual it was that the woman had pointed out the roses—but I didn't connect it to my novena. It was a while after I got back into the car and continued driving before I realized the importance of her comment. Although these were not actual fresh flowers, I recognized them as roses from Saint Therese. At that point, I got very excited because I knew that it would not be long before Kelli would find an apartment. As I kept reflecting upon the incident at the rest stop I became even more convinced that it was a sign—and then I remembered that the shirt Maddy was wearing had been a gift from Kelli herself.

That weekend, while in Maine, we visited a potential apartment for Kelli. I was certain, based on the prayers and the roses, that this was the apartment meant for her, but she wasn't comfortable with it. The only stairs to get into the apartment were very steep, and there was a pool in the backyard—not a safe place for her toddler. Mom and I discussed it, and we both agreed that it wasn't right but that something would soon come. Unbeknownst to me, my mother had been praying to Saint Therese for Kelli, too, and she had received a rose sign in her backyard—a small rose had appeared in the corner of her garden. Sure enough, within a couple of weeks, Kelli found a different apartment, which was much better suited to her needs.

The toddler referenced here is the baby that Kelli thought she was carrying, and had asked me to pray for, when we went to Medjugorje in 2002. As it turned out, she gave birth to a baby boy. Over time, I realized that Kelli was the tired, defeated woman I had a vision of in one of my very first dreams. I had this vision eight months prior to her conceiving her son. She was the one standing across the street in front of the schoolyard with a bloody finger. The bleeding wedding ring finger symbolized the future she would have as a single mother. Her fiancé, after learning that she was pregnant, abandoned her and left the state.

I've always included Kelli, her son, and her son's father in my prayers and have hoped for some kind of reconciliation for them. Although the boy's father never spoke to or saw his most beautiful, loving, talented son until almost ten years after his birth, they have finally met and are working on healing. As painful as it might be, it does demonstrate that it is never too late for anyone to have an awakening of the heart. I do not know the reason for my vision, but I do know one thing for certain: there will be an opportunity for this little boy to face the greatest challenge of all—to forgive and love the very father who abandoned him and his mother. He will have his very own way of the cross, with Jesus at his side.

Seventeen

Closure

Earlier in this book, I shared the story of moving from my childhood home in Bethel to a new city and my struggle with making the transition as I left behind all of my childhood friends. I thought about those friends for many years afterward and wondered about their lives. During one of my high school years, my father informed me that a friend of mine from Bethel, Ed, had been in a fatal car accident—he had crashed into a tree while driving. When I learned this, I was saddened and shocked, yet there was a part of me that felt very distant from him. I surmised it was because it had been several years since I had seen him, and we weren't in regular contact anymore. I knew this was a great loss of a wonderful person, but there was a part of me that almost felt numb, too. As the years passed, I thought about Ed periodically. I had fond memories of him and remembered playing Twister[1] and other games with him at one of my birthday parties. I really did hold a special place in my heart for him. When I started the practice of praying for the souls of the dead, I always included Ed's name in my prayers. Many times I wondered if he was in heaven and if my prayers were of help to him.

In the summer of 2007, my parents returned to Bethel for my mother's high school class reunion, where they spoke to a number of people whom they had not seen in years. After the event, my mother called me to say that at the reunion, a young woman approached their table and mentioned that I had been a friend of her cousin who had been killed many years ago. My mother couldn't remember the name of the woman's cousin, but I certainly knew who it was—it was my friend Ed. After years of prayers and wondering about their efficacy, I was granted this wonderful gift of validation. My eyes teared up as I said Ed's name out loud to my mother. She had no idea that her simple message would have such great significance for me. It was my sign from God that my prayers for Ed had been heard. It was also a gift in another form. Up until that moment, I had not fully grieved Ed's death, and I finally realized this. His death also represented another loss for me: the loss of the childhood friends I experienced when we left Bethel so quickly. So in a strange way, my prayers for him translated into actual healing for me. Although I had not expected it, it was closure to an open wound, and Ed was part of that.

Eighteen

Extending Spiritual Mercy

Doing God's will can be realized in many different ways, just as extending love, kindness, and mercy is possible not only through our deeds but through our thoughts and prayers. One situation helped me to understand this very profoundly. During college, I worked at a jewelry kiosk in the local mall. Across the hall was a toy store, and I became friendly with a fellow high school student named Joe. He was a year behind me in school and was one of those kids who did not really fit in with the crowd. He was shy, overweight, and a bit of a loner, and he had an inner sadness about him, something deep inside. I knew that he had a difficult life, even though he didn't share much at all about it.

Joe and I had worked together the previous summer for the city's Parks and Recreation Department. I collected money at a local swimming hole, and he was a camp counselor and would take the kids to the beach. As we talked more about our previous summer jobs, he confided in me that they would not hire him back as a counselor because he had been accused of inappropriately touching a youngster. When he told me this, I didn't have an opinion on whether it was true or false; I just remember listening but not judging him. He was very kind to me, and I developed compassion for him. Whenever he took his break at the mall, he would bring back a big soda or a snack for me. He was always very nice and I enjoyed talking with him. Toward the end of the summer when I was getting ready to head back to college, Joe stopped by my house to bring me a going-away present—a coffeemaker. I was delighted by this considerate gesture. Joe and I exchanged a few notes while I was away at college, but we eventually lost touch. I always had fond thoughts of him, however, and believed that he was a kind and loving person behind his sad exterior.

A few years after I graduated college, when I was living in the Boston area, my mother called one day to tell me a terrible and horrifying story about Joe: he had been accused of murdering his girlfriend's daughter. She shared some general details of the case. The news ripped through me and made my heart ache. I thought back to the accusations against him, years ago, at the Parks and Recreation Department. All I could think of now was that the accusation must have been true—and he must have committed this crime, too. I was repulsed by it and could not fathom the little girl's pain and how she must have suffered. At the same time, I was deeply saddened. I knew that everyone must have thought Joe was a heartless monster, but I knew him as someone else and actually felt compassion for him. Somewhere inside, there existed a sweet, kind-hearted person who used to visit me at my kiosk and bring me sodas during his break.

Years had passed where I did not think of Joe—until my spiritual awakening. In 2002, I started wondering if he was still in prison, and I even thought about going to visit him there. This idea waxed and waned, but I never forgot about him. Still, trying to see him seemed impossible; I was living in Connecticut, and he was in the Maine prison system. I did, however, start to pray for him. Then, one fall day during a trip to Maine in 2006, my family and I went to a local apple orchard where we took a hay ride and enjoyed a family day of apple picking. After filling our bags, we sat outside at a picnic table, enjoying cider and apple fritters. In the distance, I saw what appeared to be an older man—he was walking painstakingly slow and hobbling with a cane. He paused to take a breath, struggled down some steps, and then walked toward an adjacent table to join what looked to be his family. As he proceeded closer to me, I became completely engrossed by his features and was stunned by my revelation—this was not an old man; I was sure it was my old friend Joe. If this was Joe, however, he was a vision of a man destroyed not only by prison but by the destructive nature of evil acts. The state of his total physical deterioration disturbed me to the core. I was enveloped by my thoughts when my mother asked me what was going on. I explained to her what I thought I had seen. Joe had left by now and, regretfully, I had not approached him. But I told my mother that I was certain it was him. "That really shook you up," she said. She could see the pain in my eyes.

"Yes," I confirmed, feeling sick to my stomach. I felt incredibly saddened by the chain of events that resulted in

Joe's apparently devastating situation. And I felt badly that I did not summon the courage to approach and talk to him when the opportunity was there. I wanted to tell him that it was me, Amy, his friend from the past and that I wanted to learn what had happened to him. I wanted to let him know that despite it all, I did not think he was a monster. I also wanted him to know that I had been praying for him. Instead, I did nothing. I simply watched as Joe and his family got in their big white van and drove away. I deeply regretted my inaction, but the effect of seeing him was lasting.

After that day, I researched Joe's crime and was very disturbed by the details. According to the official newspaper accounts, he was found guilty of manslaughter after a five-day trial. He was convicted of suffocating the toddler after he restrained her arms to the bed with a belt, and then left her there. He was acquitted of a charge of unlawful sexual contact.[1]

My first reaction was one of complete devastation. Then, I was angry. Reading the facts in black and white made me question everything I previously thought about forgiveness. How could I possibly have sympathy or compassion for this person? I imagined the child and what she must have gone through, and then I thought of my own daughter. I also was irritated that he had seemed to make up pieces of the story during the trial, rather than admit the full truth. I concluded that he might not deserve mercy after all because he had not been honest and therefore could not really be sorrowful. But then something was triggered in me. Did I really get this concept of spiritual mercy, I asked myself, or was I just talking a good game? I looked deeply in my heart, and it occurred to me that it was not necessary for those who offend us—grievously or otherwise—to recognize or admit their own guilt in order for us to forgive and seek peace. That is not what God is asking. He is asking for forgiveness in the most extreme of situations. It is difficult to comprehend and goes against our very nature of wanting to exact justice. But if no one forgives, everyone loses out. On the other hand, if someone forgives or is merciful, some sort of peace has occurred, and there is the potential for healing.

I am not the mother of the little girl who Joe was convicted of murdering, so I can't speak to the pain of the family. Yet I do ask myself how Joe is different from me or from any of us. Is it not simply the revelation of human weakness to which we are all subject? Are we all not on that same decision continuum of love and hate, where each action either moves us closer to the hate end of the spectrum or closer to that of love?

Many people might think that Joe is not deserving of compassion or prayer because he committed an unspeakable act against an innocent child. I believe that he did commit a terrible act, and he was convicted for that. Yet I don't believe that it makes him unlovable. In the eyes of God, we are all loveable, no matter what we do; God's forgiveness is accessible to everyone. It is often difficult to be compassionate and forgiving because we know what is right and just. Forgiving people when they have committed what seems to be an unforgivable act is a lesson in spiritual growth. Because I did not need to forgive Joe for an offense against me, it was easier to see that his actions did not equal his being. I know that inside him resides a person who is not a murderer, and maybe that is what makes me want to pray for him. This is my way to show mercy to him.

I read a book called *Left to Tell* that had a powerful effect on me. It is the story of a Rwandan woman named Immaculee Ilibagiza. She survived three months in a bathroom, hidden behind a clothes dresser with seven other women during the reign of terror of the Rwandan genocide in the nineties. The assassination of the Rwandan president in 1984 was the impetus for genocide in this East African country. For over one hundred days, Hutu extremists exacted violence and mass killings against the minority Tutsi population.[2] Former friends and neighbors took part in the brutality as the Tutsis were brutalized, dehumanized, and executed. Immaculee tells the story of losing her parents, brothers, cousins, and most of the people she'd known since birth. Yet her remarkable story is that she was actually able to forgive those who butchered her family and destroyed her life and homeland. If she is capable of forgiving and finding healing in an extreme situation such as that, then perhaps I can forgive the small infractions of those around me. Perhaps I can extend even deeper compassion for those whom others may have cast aside, like Joe. Immaculee's story inspires me to do better by seeking to love more. She is one of my spiritual heroines.

One day in the spring of 2009, I was contacted through an online social networking site . . . by my old friend Joe. We exchanged e-mails and corresponded briefly. In one exchange I asked if he was at the apple orchard that day—I still wasn't completely positive—but he never replied. I am not sure where our friendship will go or what is next, but I am open to whatever path God puts before us.

Nineteen

Amy Lynn Bradley

Amy's story is in regard to a very tragic and heartbreaking matter. I debated about whether sharing this story was the right thing to do, but in the end, I decided that the related awareness outweighs my concerns about violating a private outreach made to Amy's family. Most of the story is taken from a letter I wrote in May 2006 to Ina and Ron Bradley, Amy's parents. Amy Lynn Bradley has been missing since 1998. She vanished in international waters while traveling on a Royal Caribbean Cruise Ship, *Rhapsody of the Seas*. The following details of her disappearance are highlighted from her mother's perspective on a website for missing cruise ship victims:

> Amy, our beautiful 23-year-old daughter, who had recently graduated from

college, vanished in the Caribbean on March 24, 1998.

My husband, son, Amy and I were leisurely traveling as a family during the time of her disappearance. The cruise ship was in the docking procedure in the port of Curacao, Netherlands Antilles.

Amy had left her cabin during the early morning hours of March 24th, taking her cigarettes and lighter with her. Obviously, she had not intended to be gone for very long, as she did not wear her shoes.

There are many, many unanswered questions surrounding Amy's disappearance . . . Who was she meeting at this early hour? Why would she take her cigarettes and lighter? Neither the cruise line nor government authorities have provided any answers. At this time, neither of these entities has made or is making proactive efforts of inquiries regarding our daughter's mysterious disappearance.

The summary concludes with the following plea:

Since the time of her disappearance, we have continued to search for our daughter and seek answers for finding her. It is be-

lieved that there are certain individuals in
the Caribbean, and possibly even in South
America, who have knowledge of Amy's
disappearance. All we want is the safe return
of our daughter. We continue to plead with
anyone who may have knowledge of her
whereabouts.[1]

Ina and Ron Bradley have been searching for their
daughter since that day in 1998 when she disappeared and
have never given up their quest to find her. In 2005, they
were on a television talk show to discuss their situation. In
fact, that is how I learned about her case. It was during the
time when a teenage girl, Natalee Holloway, went missing
in Aruba. Her case flooded the headlines and also brought
attention to other missing persons, which is when Amy's
story re-surfaced in the media. After hearing about her, and
after deep prayer and reflection, I decided to reach out to her
family in a letter. I had never before done anything like this
and was a bit self-conscious, but Amy was on my mind, and
I could not shake her story. I wrote a letter and sent it to the
Bradleys, not knowing how it might be received, yet I knew
I needed to make a supportive gesture to this family. Below
is part of a letter I sent to Ina and Ron Bradley in May 2006.

Dear Mr. and Mrs. Bradley,

My name is Amy Boucher. I am thirty-six
years old, live in Connecticut, and am a wife
and mother of a two-year-old girl. For some
time now I have contemplated writing this

letter to you. We don't know each other, and I have never met your daughter, Amy. I do not have information pertaining to Amy, yet in some way, I feel a special connection to her. I learned of Amy's story back in 2005 during one of the news broadcasts related to the missing Alabama teen, Natalee Holloway. I do not recall the exact date but it was probably in November, around the time that the Dr. Phil show aired, on which you both appeared to talk about Amy. Although I was already developing an interest in your daughter's story, I became even more interested after I learned that a picture surfaced that could be Amy. I kept thinking about Amy, wondering what she must be going through, and imagining the details of how she might be living. I couldn't stop thinking about her and regularly started to search the Internet to learn more about her disappearance and for information and updates on her whereabouts. The more I learned, the more distraught I became—on behalf of Amy and on behalf of you, her parents and family. I was angry and outraged at the injustice perpetrated against you and your family. Before long, I felt the intense desire to do *something* to be helpful and aid in the situation, but I thought, what could I possibly do to help Amy or your family?

In late January, I finally decided that I had to do something constructive with my

SEASON OF THE ROSE

concern for Amy. It occurred to me that God might be speaking to me through these repeated thoughts and that I could make some kind of difference through prayer. Feeling frustrated at my helplessness, I began to pray during the month of January. I am not sure if you practice a particular faith and if so, you might even know what I am going to share, but in the absence of knowing about your faith, I will tell you a little about how I decided to pray for Amy. I am Catholic, and as part of the Catholic tradition, the faithful often pray to saints, individuals who have lived on this earth and have demonstrated in some extraordinary way their love of Jesus Christ and who are known also to perform miracles for those on earth who pray to them. Catholics also pray what is known as novenas—nine days of continuous prayers to a saint or spiritual figure, where we ask these saints to intercede for us before Jesus regarding very specific favors. As part of my prayers for Amy, I decided to pray to one of my favorite saints, Saint Therese of Lisieux. This special saint is well known for sending a special sign of roses to those who pray to her, as recognition that she has heard their prayers and often as a sign that those prayers have or will be answered. I had previously said several novenas to Saint Therese [for other issues], and each time, my prayers were answered, and I received roses. Once, a priest walked up to me in church and presented me with a rose. Another time, I passed by a rose bush in full bloom in the cold of autumn. I also received very specific responses and direction after my novenas.

I believe in Saint Therese and knew that she would hear me. I had also learned of another saint, Saint Rita. . . . she is known as the Saint of the Impossible. I thought that if Amy needed anything, she needed help from the Saint of the Impossible. I do have to admit, however, that I had some trepidation over praying to Saint Rita. Since she isn't known to provide any visible sign such as roses, how would I know if she was hearing my prayers? I worried about this a bit but then realized that signs were not necessary. All I needed to do was to have faith and trust in God that my prayers would be heard.

In my prayers, I asked that Amy would be returned to her parents and family in this year, 2006. I wanted to be very specific in my request, as I have learned that God wants us to ask for exactly what we need. He already knows our heart but wants us to ask, so I did; and continued praying for Amy throughout January. In February, on Valentine's Day, my husband and I went out to dinner. We were escorted to our table, and on the table was a beautiful bouquet of roses. At first, I thought that the roses were part of the restaurant's décor but soon noticed that there was a card in the flowers, and that the flowers were for me. My husband had arrived at the restaurant before me and orchestrated this beautiful surprise. . . . I later realized that these roses could have been my roses from St. Therese, but actually started to doubt whether that was true. After all, it was Valentine's Day, and wasn't it common for women to receive roses on this day? . . . I knew that praying for Amy was surely helpful, but I wanted more confirmation that these very important prayers were being heard. . . .

I thought of writing to you several times and letting you know that I was praying for [Amy] and to extend my support. I also wanted to send to you the prayer cards of St. Therese and St. Rita. . . . I kept meaning to write to you but the time never seemed right, and I was not exactly sure what to say. In the meantime, I kept checking the Amy Lynn Bradley links on the Internet, hoping for an update with good news . . .

In March, as we entered into the solemn and reflective season of Lent, a time when Catholics and other Christians typically give something up or make some sacrifice for the forty days leading to Easter, I decided that I would pray every day for Amy. I decided to pray a special prayer, called the Chaplet of Divine Mercy, which is said on the rosary. This is also a very special prayer that Jesus revealed to a Polish nun, known now as Saint Faustina. He told Saint Faustina that *"through the chaplet you will obtain everything, if what you want is compatible with my will."* At the beginning of the Lenten season, I was praying very specifically that "Amy Lynn Bradley will be returned to her parents and family in this year, 2006." I then added prayers for Amy's perseverance and strength, and prayers that she might not give up hope to be rescued or released. As the season progressed, I began to add prayers for others—for all men, women, and children held against their will or held in captivity. As the end of Lent approached, I added other parts to the prayers. I prayed that Amy's captors and all captors holding people against their will would experience a change of heart. I also prayed that these captors might be brought to justice.

On Wednesday of Holy Week, the week leading up to Easter Sunday, I was driving to work, praying the chaplet for Amy and suddenly came to understand with absolute clarity the importance of adding in the prayer for a change of heart for her captors. I knew with certainty that I needed to pray not only for Amy, the innocent victim, but for those who are in great spiritual need—those who do not yet know God—so that their hearts may be converted and be enlightened by his truths. I also came to understand that my prayers for justice were misaligned; that although justice is a natural human desire, real justice is out of our hands and will be done according to God's will. The fact that I came to this realization during Lent had a great impact on me. I was reminded that Jesus was condemned, scourged, pressed to carry his own cross, and then crucified by his own people. It was not fair. Justice according to this world did not happen. But God's justice always prevails.

On this same Wednesday I missed the noontime Mass . . . I often attend. Since it was Holy Week and I wanted to go to Mass every day, I decided to drive twenty minutes to a church in a nearby town that I hadn't been to in over two years. . . . As I walked into the foyer of the church, I noticed a table to the right of the doorway. On the table were different materials—information about the Easter season, prayer cards, and other miscellaneous items. Immediately, my eyes were drawn to two prayer cards that were standing upright on the small table. One of them was the prayer card of St. Therese and the other was the prayer card of St. Rita. These were the exact prayer cards that I had been using for Amy! . . . What is the chance that on this day, I would decide to go to a church . . . to find the two very special prayer cards . . . standing upright, as if just waiting for me to arrive? Upon seeing the cards, all of the doubts that had accumulated about whether the roses were really a sign or if the saints were hearing my prayers immediately dissipated. . . . Throughout the Mass, I was quite emotional, tearful, and overwhelmed . . . All this time I was worried about my prayers being heard. How would *I* know if the saints were responding? How would *I* know when the prayers had been heard? It never occurred to me that I might receive a message on behalf of someone else. Yet in an instant, it became clear to me that the cards were there not for my benefit but for yours. This was a gift, given by God to you and your family, to let you know that he hears your prayers and sends his great love to you. I am sincerely humbled to be able to share this special message of hope with you.

None of us knows what the future holds. We can only hope and pray that it includes Amy's returning to your family. Whatever it does hold, however, know that God is with you and with Amy. Do not give up. Persevere. Amy is truly in God's hands.

If there is anything that I may do for you and your family, please do not hesitate to contact me. . . . May God bless you and your family.

I enclosed the two prayer cards found in the church that day and sent them with my letter. The letter was met with warmth and appreciation from Amy's mother. We later exchanged e-mails, and she sent me photos of Amy and a special key chain with Amy's picture. It currently hangs from a lamp in our office to remind us of the importance to continue praying for Amy and her family. We still have no further information about Amy as of this writing, but I have not lost faith that my prayers will be answered. One never knows how God will work. Maybe someone who has influence over Amy's situation will read this book. Maybe someone else will take up her cause and either begin to pray for her or increase their existing prayers. The important part of this is to realize that the power is not only in God's manifestation of help but also in how we determine to help others here on earth. There is great comfort provided to others when they know that friends, family, or even strangers are praying for them and care for them.

Amy's situation has had a major impact on my personal prayer life. Since learning of her story and praying for her during that Lenten season, I now pray regularly for men, women, and children held against their will, and for God to put into motion the circumstances necessary that will free these individuals from captivity. I feel a special calling toward this group of people, and Amy is the one who inspired this in me. Since I believe deeply in the power of prayer, I know that mine are making a difference.

Keychain with photo of Amy Lynn Bradley given to me by her mother.

Twenty
A Child's Dying Wish

For the most part, Amy was the first stranger I prayed for, but certainly not the last. One day, I learned of a situation with a little girl who was in the hospital, dying of cancer. Her father had been in a military prison as a result of a drug violation. The little girl did not have much time to live, and her dying wish was to have her father by her side. The prison authorities were reticent to let the father leave prison. For whatever reason, there were complications with letting him go to his daughter's bedside. I did not know the exact details of the situation, but my heart was in shreds for the little girl. I read the story of this innocent child and simply could not tolerate the potential of her not seeing her father before she died. In an effort to affect the situation, I decided to say a novena. This time, I chose to pray to Saint Jude who is often associated with little children. We see his name regularly in the well-known establishment St. Jude's Children's Hospital. He is also known as a worker of miracles and the saint of lost causes.[1] I did not think of this when I decided to appeal to him. I only thought of the promise that whoever says this specific prayer nine times a day, for nine days, and leaves nine copies of the prayer in church each day will receive his/her request on or before the eighth day and that this prayer "has never been known to fail." I prayed diligently and fervently for the little girl. Each day, I checked the Internet for updates on her status. This prayer was filled with so much passion that my body almost ached with sympathy for the family. I kept questioning what kind of society we live in that restricts a loving parent from seeing his dying child. What rules or guidelines override this basic level of decency? Where was the mercy? This truly bothered me. I was haunted by this cruelty, especially because this child could not have done anything to deserve this treatment. All she wanted was to see her father before she died.

On day eight of the novena, after I had left the copies of my prayers in church, I returned home and checked the Internet. What I found sent a wave of relief through my body. Just as the novena promised, my petition was answered on the eighth day. This little girl's father had finally been allowed to leave prison to visit his daughter for one last time. It was reported that the little girl died in her hospital room only hours after her father left her bedside. My eyes welled with tears. This little girl, who was unable to verbally communicate, held on long enough to feel the presence of her father by her side before she left this world and passed into eternity. It was a beautiful testament to the power of the human spirit and the mystery of the soul. We are more than our physical beings. There is more to this world than the physical aspect of our nature, and this girl's plight epitomized this.

I was relieved that this child received what she longed for, and I was thankful for Saint Jude's intervention. I realize that people all over the country and probably the world were praying for this little girl, but I am certain that Saint Jude pulled through on this one. As part of the novena, I repeatedly prayed: "Oh, come to my aid that I may praise the mercies of God. All my life I will be grateful to you and will be your faithful servant until I can thank you in heaven."[2] I hope that by sharing this story, many people will reach out to Saint Jude and harness the beautiful power of God's love through this special saint.

THE
HARVEST

"Dear children! In this time of grace, when nature also prepares to give the most beautiful
colors of the year, I call you, little children, to
open your hearts to God the Creator for Him
to transform and mold you in His image, so
that all the good which has fallen asleep in
your hearts may awaken to a new life and a
longing towards eternity. Thank you for having responded to my call."[1]

~Mary's Message of February 25, 2010~

Twenty-One

More Signs

*People often ask me if I still experience unusual and su-*pernatural things. I do but in slightly different ways. I now realize that I had to experience those initial striking events in order to awaken my spirituality. I am still touched by God on a regular basis and am the recipient of tremendous graces. Yet I believe that God is always with us and is accessible to all of us. We simply need to seek Him out and, when He speaks to us, be open to hearing His response or call. As it says in the Bible in Matthew 7:7, "Ask and it will be given to you; seek and you will find; knock and the door will be opened to you."[1] I revel in the daily graces and inspirations, sometimes smaller but of no less impact than those I initially experienced.

One of the times I experienced another unusual event in my environment had to do with our new house.

After Steve and I bought our first home in 2003, we spent a lot of time organizing it, adjusting to parenthood, and busying ourselves with work, soccer, and other activities. One night, Steve and I were sitting in our dining room, admiring a new piece of furniture that we had recently purchased. We talked incessantly about various remodeling projects and what types of things we would do next to improve the house. Shortly after our conversation ended, I walked upstairs, and as I reached the top of the stairs, I heard a loud bang. It sounded as though a large box had been dropped. I called down the stairs to Steve. He said he heard the noise, too, but did not know what it was. I walked back down the stairs into the living room to look around. I glanced up at a shelf and noticed that the picture of us, the same picture that had flown off of the radiator in our previous apartment, wasn't on the shelf. I said to Steve, "Don't even tell me." Together, we discovered the picture on the back of the couch. It had not fallen on the hard floor. It had not cracked. Instead, it had landed gently on the back of the couch, yet the sound echoed all the way upstairs, as if an object of great weight had fallen to the floor. We both needed to hear the loud bang in order to get our attention. How a picture falling against a couch creates the sound of a large box falling cannot be explained. What was important was that we recognized this as another sign, another grace, that we had something to do together and that we needed to remain strong together in order to fulfill God's will.

We had been under a lot of stress as a couple, trying to balance our new life and all of our commitments. We both felt extreme tension with one another but really never talked about it. This night, we cleared the air and agreed that we would work harder together to help each other and make our lives more manageable. We also agreed that we needed to correct our direction and stop focusing on materialistic things, such as renovating our house. We could do some of the things that we wanted with the house, but that should not take precedence over what we thought we were supposed to be doing. What we concluded was that I should write this book, with Steve's help, guidance, and encouragement. Although I had been the recipient of the most direct incidents, we did ascertain that this is a mission for both of us—that it was ours together. We agreed that, for whatever reason, we had been given these experiences and they were to be shared, not harbored. The message wasn't ours to keep but God's to share. It was, after all, a call from God to *all* of his children.

After we agreed that we needed to write the book, I spent a lot of time avoiding the actual work of writing. I had excuse after excuse—too tired, the baby, not motivated, not sure people would be receptive, and so forth. Many months after the picture incident in the house, I entered into a very brief but very intense prayer. I was frustrated with myself and tired of wondering if I should write this book. I prayed intently to the Lord and asked Him to send me a very specific sign if it was His desire that I write this book. I said the prayer, asked my favor, and went on with my activities of the day. Later that evening, a family friend named John stopped by and told me that he had been to a park earlier that day to quietly think and meditate. He thanked me for a pocket prayer card I had given him a while back and said he used it at the park that day. I could not remember which prayer card I had given him, but as he pulled it out to show me, I noticed it was a prayer card from Medjugorje with a picture of the Blessed Virgin Mary, a card I'd had blessed while on our trip there. I had forgotten that I had even given it to him. I smiled broadly and thought that this might be my sign.

I asked John which park he had visited. He told me he'd gone to one in a nearby city, and he'd chosen it because there have been reported apparitions of the Virgin Mary there. Purportedly, people have observed her in between two trees, and a spontaneous shrine has been erected. People go there in hopes of seeing a vision of her, as well as to pray and meditate. When I heard that, I was filled with uncontrollable excitement—I'd finally received my sign that the book must indeed be written.

As always, things are never finished according to my own time, and writing the book seemed to go on endlessly. Finally, when I reached a point where I thought the book was in fairly good shape, Steve and I became more diligent about finding a way to publish it. Steve's soccer teammate had recently written a book and suggested that we join the Connecticut Author's and Publisher's Association (CAPA). We researched it and determined that it was a good resource. In the fall of 2007, we paid our dues and joined the organization. Steve and I attended several monthly meetings and began to network and learn about the publishing industry. We quickly learned that it was much more complicated than we had thought, and that the odds of securing a big publishing house and writing a *New York Times* best-seller were slim to none. One of the highlights of CAPA, however, is its annual conference, "CAPA University" (CAPA-U). This is one of the most revered events for local writers. It is essentially a conference with different sessions aimed at helping authors perfect their manuscripts. The highlight of the event, however, is the opportunity for each member to meet with either a literary agent or an editor. The member must select in advance with whom he/she wants to meet, and only one meeting is permitted. Steve and I were excited to attend. Because we both are members, we were in the unique position to meet with two different people for the same book.

Part of the requirement for scheduling a meeting was to write a query letter, which introduces the theme or intent of the manuscript to the editor or agent. There is a generally accepted format used for this process, but being new to the entire publishing industry, Steve and I did not exactly know how to complete this letter. Fortunately, the president of CAPA was extremely gracious and took numerous e-mails and calls from us as we pressed for clarity on exactly what was expected. Still, we were getting nervous, especially since we were heading for a family vacation with Steve's parents in Florida. As it turned out, we actually finished the letter on our first full day in Florida. Neither of us wanted to do this on our vacation, but we knew we had to get it done. We took turns trying to finesse the letter, referencing ones we found on the Internet and in a publishing book we'd purchased.

I got tired and frustrated and needed a break. I told Steve and his parents that I needed to spend some time by myself for a while. No one objected, so I went down to the pool, grabbed a lounge chair, stretched my legs out, adjusted my baseball cap, and leaned back to relax. The sun was warm, and I sighed as I slid back in the lounger. The letter writing had tired me, but I was also just fatigued, as I was in my first trimester of pregnancy with my second daughter, Maisie. As I sat back in my chair, I noticed a plane weaving about, doing aerials, preparing to write words in the sky. I wondered if some lucky girl was going to get a marriage proposal. I watched carefully as the plane gracefully sketched the first letter, "J." I watched as the plane formed the next letter, trying to guess what the girl's name might be. And then it formed another letter, and another . . . and I could not believe what I was seeing. In the sky, before my very eyes, were the letters J - E - S - U - S. This was unbelievable! I stared at the sky in disbelief. Yes, hovering over my head, in giant cloud-like letters, was the unmistakable name of Jesus.

I was so excited that I bolted from my seat and ran as fast as I could back to the resort unit. I wanted desperately for Steve to see this before it vanished from the sky. Pregnant and winded, I ran up six flights of stairs and flew through the door. "Hurry!" I called out. "You won't believe this!" I directed everyone to the screened-in porch, and pointed to the sky, where the letters were still visible. We pulled out the camera and quickly took a picture. Gene, Steve's father, turned to me and said, "I don't think you need any help with your book." We all laughed and marveled at the sign—this time, a literal sign in the sky. Jesus was sending us His encouragement. If Jesus wanted this book published, it would happen, CAPA-U or no CAPA-U.

A couple of weeks later, we attended the meeting and met with two agents, one of whom took an interest. We also met other professionals and received a referral for an editor. Although neither of the agent leads materialized, we did secure an editor through the process and worked with

Sky-written "Jesus" seen from the screened-in porch of our resort room.

her on the first formal edits of the book. She added tremendous value, and Steve and I believe that we had exactly the type of editing we needed to take the book to the next phase in its development.

Twenty-Two

The Blazing Warrior

One of the initial concerns I had about writing this book was that people might not believe my story. After all, many people claim to have visions and receive messages—some more credible than others. Sincerely believing that God's hand is in this book, however, I concluded that it would reach those it needed to touch, regardless of my own ability to prove or validate the facts. I still believe that is the case, but God put into motion some special circumstances that helped take the mysteries to a new level, involving people other than just my family and me.

Once I started sharing an initial version of the book with a few people and seeking feedback on what was missing, I gained confidence that it was almost ready to be published. In the back of my mind, doubts still lingered as to how I could get the point across to others that this really wasn't just a story about me and that it was real. One night while on the phone with my mother, she shared some interesting news that quickly became linked to this book. She received a call from a family member who had owned the haunted house that we rented in my youth. The family member wanted to learn more about our experiences when we lived there. A friend of hers had recently spent a night in the house and had a haunting experience of her own. The woman, while sleeping, was awakened by a startling sound. When she opened her eyes she saw a dark figure of a man standing at the side of her bed. He was bent over, looking down at her. Alarmed and terrified, she sat up in haste and the figure disappeared. She was convinced it was a ghost. After twenty-six years of my being absolutely certain that something had happened there, I finally received validation from an external source. Indeed, there were spirits, ghosts, or a presence in that house when I was there, and apparently, some sort of activity still persists. At first, this became very important to me. I felt vindicated and knew this was the proof I needed to quiet skeptics who might doubt my story. Yet again, Jesus made sure to point me to the source of all truth. He was about to show me something more profound and directly related to the authenticity and power of Medjugorje that could only be arranged by God, as another form of encouragement to take Mary's messages seriously and with trust.

In 2006, I took a new job at a local company and began a different chapter of my life. This permitted Steve to stay at home with our daughter, Madeline, and to take time to develop a website for the book and to look for editors and publishers. We believed that this move was a critical piece of our overall plan and that God was granting us this grace, giving us time to prepare the book for publication.

Not long after I joined the new company, I attended a training event. At the beginning, the facilitator conducted an icebreaker exercise to help participants get to know one another. She asked us to share our name, how long we had been at the company, what role we were in, and a little-known secret about ourselves. I decided to share with my group of peers that I was writing a book. I was very vague about the content and only said that I was writing a story about my journey to a small village in Bosnia-Herzegovina. This was one of the first times I ever spoke to people outside of my small circle of family and friends about the book. Part of me knew that I had to start sharing if it was ever going to become a reality, yet it still made me a little uncomfortable.

During one of the breaks, a colleague—a woman named Karen—approached me and seemed intrigued by my writing a book. After class ended, we walked out together, back to the main building across the street. She asked me about the book; she wanted to know in more detail what it was about. I'd seen Karen occasionally at the noon Mass in the cathedral near work, and sensed I might be able to open up a little to her. I told her that I was writing a story about Medjugorje, where there were visions of the Virgin Mary, and that Mary was sending messages for the world to return to God to achieve greater peace. It was similar, I told her, to the events in Lourdes, France, and Fatima, Portugal—other locations where Mary had appeared to children in the past, sending them the same urgent messages for the world to return to God. Although Karen was Catholic, she'd never heard of Medjugorje, but said she would research it.

She told me that my book sounded interesting and that it seemed like a book from which many people would benefit.

Over the next six to eight months, I saw Karen periodically but never had a direct conversation with her or spoke to her again about the book. We were assigned to the same project at work but had fairly limited contact because the group was so large. One day, almost a year later in September, I woke up in a great mood and was looking forward to the day. This was refreshing, as my work environment at the time was very stressful and a source of extreme frustration for me. On this day, however, I knew that my calendar was clear at noon and I was determined to make it to the cathedral for Mass. As I was driving to work, Karen entered my mind, and I decided that I would contact her to ask if she wanted to go with me.

When I arrived in the office, the first thing I did was send her an e-mail, which I sent around 9:30 with the subject line "Mass." A couple of hours passed, and I did not hear from her. I wondered if she had received my message. Just before noon, the phone rang, and it was Karen. She told me that she could not believe that I had e-mailed her. She thought it was quite ironic that I contacted her, because after more than a year of not really communicating with each other, it just happened that she was planning to approach me on something this very week. A very close friend of hers, Cassidy, was out of work on disability as a result of a resurgence of breast cancer and was undergoing chemotherapy treatments. Cassidy told her that she had a mystical experience related to the Virgin Mary that was powerful and moving. Although Karen did not know the details of her experience, she remembered that I had been writing a book about Mary and thought I might be able to help her in some way. She did not know the details of my book nor what I had been through, but felt very strongly that her friend and I should get together.

Karen and I talked for a while and were both amazed that we had been thinking of each other at the same time. We knew somehow that something greater than us was bringing us together. For all intents and purposes, we were strangers to one another but linked somehow in this larger plan of God's. She suggested that maybe I was supposed to share my book with Cassidy or that maybe her experience had something to do with writing my book. Karen asked if I would meet with Cassidy to listen to her story and to possibly share mine. I was honored by the request and responded affirmatively. If someone needed me spiritually, I would be there.

We arranged for the three of us to get together after work during the third week in September, about two weeks from the time of our initial contact. I had been putting off the tedious process of making changes to my book; this meeting was the impetus to finally do that. The day before we planned our get-together, I took a personal day from work. I wrote for twelve hours, barely stopping to eat or to do anything else. Somehow, I knew that I had to share a draft copy with both Karen and Cassidy. I was so touched that they trusted me enough to bring me into the fold of this special situation that I, in return, trusted them to read a draft of my book. Then I realized something: it was not really about us. What we were doing wasn't about trusting each other but about trusting in God through each other. None of us knew the significance of the meeting or why we were being brought together, but we all sensed that something special was happening.

One Tuesday evening after work, Karen and I took separate cars to Cassidy's home in a nearby town. Since I did not know Cassidy or what state she would be in from her cancer treatment, I was a bit hesitant about the visit. But as I pulled into her condo complex, all doubt was removed, and I knew I was right where I should be. As I turned the corner, I noticed a statue of the Blessed Virgin Mary on the front lawn of her neighbor's house. It seems that Mary shows up wherever she is needed and always at the right time. Little did I know that she had made her presence known to Cassidy in a way that would be far more powerful than I could ever have imagined.

Karen soon arrived, too, with pizza and salad, and we sat down to dinner, sharing some personal history and getting to know one another. Before long, the conversation turned to Mary, and Cassidy asked me to share some of my experiences. As I told her my story, I became very engrossed in the details and, as always, began to feel the excitement and intensity generated when reflecting upon the awesome path of enlightenment afforded me. I realized that we could be there for many hours if I continued like this, so I tried to summarize the story, bringing out only the important details.

Then Cassidy described her own remarkable encounter with Mary. While undergoing chemotherapy a few months earlier, she'd had a very difficult day. Her only son had left town for a family reunion, and she was feeling extremely ill. She gathered all her strength and called a close family friend, saying she needed to get to the emergency room, and she needed to get there fast. In the back of her mind, she sensed the magnitude of what was happening. She felt that she was barely hanging on to her life and did not want to be alone. Her friend arrived and quickly transported her to the emergency room. She was immediately admitted to the intensive care unit, and the doctors began to gather around. Due to her extreme condition, she was also administered her last rites—a sacrament of the church, also known as anointing of the sick—given by a priest for those who are dying.

Cassidy lay in the hospital room, slipping in and out of consciousness. When she was awake, she prayed. Over the years, she had developed a particular devotion to St. Joseph, the earthly father of Jesus and Mary's husband. Cassidy had been in and out of the church at different points in her life, with different levels of commitment and involvement. She had experienced a divorce, left the church, and returned periodically. Somehow, however, she maintained her affinity to St. Joseph and often called upon him in prayer. On this day, however, she said that she had an urge to pray directly to Mary instead. She said, "There is just something about the love of a mother."

Within a short time after calling out to Mary, Cassidy experienced something truly mystical. As she lay in her hospital bed, clinging to her life, she suddenly saw the image of Mary standing over the bed. Although she could not see her whole body, she was able to see her face. Mary raised her hands above Cassidy and moved them up and down the entire length of her body. Light emanated from her hands, producing an energy that penetrated Cassidy with warmth. She felt an incredible healing force radiating through her entire body. She was totally enveloped by

Mary's gentle but powerful presence. Mary did not transmit the docile, passive image that she had expected but instead projected a strong, powerful, persistent force. Cassidy described her as being a "warrior for her children." Mary worked over her body for what seemed like two to three hours and at one point, left her bedside and approached the doctor who was standing in the corner of the room, looking down at paperwork and test results. As she stood behind the doctor, she gently placed both of her hands on the oncologist's head and stayed in that position for an undetermined amount of time. Cassidy closed her eyes and faded out of consciousness.

When she awoke some time later, she was still considered to be in a critical state but said that she felt more at ease. A doctor approached her and asked if she would like to speak to a chaplain, as there was no Catholic priest on site. Cassidy said that she would like to talk to anyone who was available. Within a few minutes, a non-denominational female chaplain came to her bedside. Cassidy was happy to see her and relieved that there was someone with whom she could share her story. "You might not believe this," she said, "but I just spent the last few hours with the Blessed Mother." The chaplain looked at her and smiled gently. She took Cassidy's hand and said, "Well, then you are going to be very happy with what I brought you." Still in a fatigued state, she watched the chaplain curiously as she reached into her pocket and took out two small gifts. The first was a beautiful rosary, the trademark sign of Mary, and the second was a tiny pocket prayer card. On the top of the prayer card was the word *Medjugorje*.

During her extended stay in the hospital, Cassidy

grew stronger as she battled her cancer. Remarkably, after barely clinging to life, she showed progress and turned the corner toward recovery. For someone who had thought she was going to die the day she entered the hospital, this was nothing short of a miracle. Although she stated that she wasn't completely "out of the woods," she attributed healing during this time directly to Mary.

For several months after our initial meeting, Cassidy and I continued to exchange e-mails and communicate via Karen. I learned that she had gained enough strength to extend her daily walk to twenty minutes and was even able to attend Mass on a daily basis. She shared with me that she was exploring writing a book to help cancer survivors like herself. She said she wanted people to know that they did not have to go through the experience alone. I asked her if we could get together at some point in the future to talk about how I thought her story fit into my book. I was sensitive to her situation and did not want to push it, but she said that she would let me know a good time, after she met with her doctor. I looked forward to seeing her again and let her know how much her miraculous story touched me and had the potential to touch so many others.

I received a call from Karen in March, on Holy Thursday, the Thursday before Easter. She informed me that Cassidy was not doing well. In fact, her doctors said that there was nothing more that they could do for her. She was at home, with her family and friends, and had asked Karen to inform me of this news. She asked her to relay that she had not forgotten me and asked me to continue to pray for her. I was overwhelmed with sadness at the news. After work that day, I drove to a nearby church and stood in front of a beautiful statue of Mary. Tears filled my eyes as my grief surfaced, and I recited a special rosary for Cassidy. At times, I'd thought that her miraculous experience would lead to a full recovery, yet there was a part of me that knew this would not be the case. Over the next week, I continued to pray for her by including her in a Divine Mercy novena, the nine-day prayer that Jesus dictated to Saint Faustina. On a sunny spring day in 2008, Cassidy died in her home, surrounded by her family and friends who had kept a vigil by her side. In speaking with Karen, I learned that she seemed to be at peace prior to her death, ever since Mary's appearance. She was able to hold on for the celebration of her son's thirtieth birthday. What a blessing.

I attended visiting hours and the funeral on the following Saturday. It was held at a local church and it was a beautiful service. I kept struggling with balancing the intimacy of my personal relationship with Cassidy and the greater and bolder impact I knew that our connection represented. After all, we hadn't known each other very long and by most standards, not very well at all. It was not until she was well advanced in her disease that I had the privilege of getting to know her the evening we had dinner and shared our experiences. But the true beauty lies in the fact that God's love knows no time or boundaries. His love is not limited to the contexts and confines of this world. Cassidy and I did not need to know each other in the human context to connect in a deep and intense spiritual way. We simply had to extend our hearts in love, even if it was just for a moment.

At the funeral Mass, I prepared to receive Holy Communion by reflecting deeply in prayer. I rose from the pew, entered into the aisle, and approached the priest to receive the host. "Ave Maria" (the Hail Mary prayer in Latin) was radiating in song throughout the church as Mass participants made their way to Communion. The sun shone brightly through the vaulted glass ceiling of the church, illuminating the path down the aisle. If ever there was a time when I thought that only God could create a moving moment like this, it was now. I bowed before the priest before accepting the host, and as I looked up, I looked directly into the eyes of a familiar face. The priest presiding over Cassidy's funeral was the only priest who had ever heard any part of my story, the one who brought me back into the church in a loving and nonjudgmental way. This was the priest who guided Steve and me through pre-marriage counseling and helped us both so much. At this point, I knew that somehow things had come full circle. After seven years of struggle, strife, reflection, and growth, I knew I was getting close to the beginning of the next chapter in my life, a major component of which would be sharing my story more broadly with others.

As for Cassidy, I cannot imagine the impact that her story will have upon other people in this world. Her impact on me is profound and our connection through "our Blessed Mother," as she referred to her, is deep and everlasting. She brought me inspiration and hope—inspiration to complete my manuscript and hope that people would see beyond my own experiences. The non-denominational chaplain also provided light in a time of need to Cassidy, and she did it in a way that crossed religious boundaries. She demonstrated the true meaning of respect and love for one's neighbor.

The real story is an invitation and opportunity to respond to the deep, penetrating love of God. Cassidy not only responded to that invitation but also gave me the great gift of seeing Jesus and Mary work powerfully through her. God gives us Mary through the church as well as throughout the world in her appearances at places such as Medjugorje; Lourdes, France; Fatima, Portugal; Knock, Ireland; Kibeho, Rwanda; and Guadalupe, Mexico. He gives us Mary to call us back to Him, and this call is for *everyone*. God does not discriminate. He simply extends his love to us in all possible ways.

Twenty-Three

The Pope

Pope Benedict XVI, the world leader of the Roman Catho-
lic Church, was planning an apostolic visit to the United
States in the spring of 2008. In early winter of that year, in
anticipation of his visit, parishioners at my church learned
that a limited number of people from various parishes
across the country would be able to attend the papal Mass
at Yankee Stadium in New York City in April. Our parish
priest encouraged anyone interested to sign up on the regis-
tration list in the front of the church. I signed up.

In March, I received a call from a nun at our parish—
I had been selected to attend the Mass. I was thrilled and
thanked her for the great news. I was aware what a special gift this was, but as the trip grew closer, I learned just
how fortunate I was to have a ticket. Apparently, each local parish was afforded only eight tickets. People all around

the country were eager to get close to the Pope, to catch a glimpse of him during this historic visit, and the only way to get into this Mass was to have a ticket issued in advance. Security was tight, and each attendee's name and identification was documented in advance of the event. Interest in his visit was high. In fact, roughly half a million people would be lucky enough to see him at some point during his journey.

The week before we were scheduled to attend the Mass, I had still not received my ticket or any information relative to the trip. Finally, on Thursday, just days before the event, I received a second call from the nun. She informed me that, although my name was on the list of attendees and had been submitted as the very first name, somehow they left me off the list and only sent seven tickets back to the parish. I was without a ticket! The nun, however, assured me that she had addressed the situation. She said that they were holding a ticket for me at the Archdiocese of Hartford. On Friday, I drove there and picked up my golden ticket (yes, it really was golden!).

The "golden" admission ticket to the Pope's mass at Yankee Stadium in New York.

I was so grateful to have that eighth and final ticket from our parish. The fact that there was confusion over it and that I actually received a ticket made me even more grateful and appreciative of all the spiritual gifts and privileges I have been given. I was going to see the Pope!

A small group of pilgrims gathered at a local church and traveled via bus to New York that Sunday morning to celebrate Mass with the Holy Father. It was a magical day for me. Being in the same arena as this wonderfully holy and humble man was a once-in-a-lifetime opportunity. I sat in a stadium seat, high above the field, and looked out on to the procession as the Pope entered Yankee Stadium. I watched in awe as the "Pope-mobile" traveled around the stadium, and I waved my yellow Vatican flag in loving support of the Pope and the church. All of the challenges of the church, all of the criticism and scandal it has been plagued by in recent years seemed ever distant from this faith-rich scene. I felt like I was part of a community, that this was an extension of my home, and I was proud to be standing upright, waving my flag in unity with my brothers and sisters of faith.

The Pope's overriding message for his visit was clear. He was on a mission, calling for a "spiritual renewal," a reawakening of Catholics in America. The Pope's message resonated with me. I had been awakened back in 2001 and was growing more and more committed to the spiritual journey every day.

Twenty-Four
Everyday Spirituality

Almost ten years since my story began to unfold, I finally was wrapping up the details of my experience. When writing this book I frequently felt elated and excited, thinking about how positive these messages are. I sincerely hoped that people would feel inspired by their beauty. Then my enthusiasm was tempered by the reality of a world in turmoil. People are hurting. There are wars, destruction of the family, kidnappings, murder, starvation, and genocide.

Consider the situation in World War II: Hitler's Germany and the extermination of the Jews. It still happens today—people slaughtered their neighbors in vicious ways during the Rwandan genocide. Think about the Bosnian War, where the same thing happened in the early 1990s, and look at the atrocities in Darfur in the western Sudan, where genocide has been occurring since 2003. Look at individual situations where children are abused and abandoned or where violence exists in the family. Think about sex and prostitution rings, where children, women, and men are stolen and held against their will. Think about people starving while others live in excess, and inhabitants left to fend for themselves in areas affected by natural disasters. Reflect upon corporate and political corruption, where leaders abuse their positions, driven by the lust for money and power.

We gasp at the horror of the atrocities that others perpetrate as we watch television and read news reports. We wonder how individuals and groups can be so horrible to others. It is easy to claim from a distance that we would never act that way, that we would never treat people badly, and that we would never harm our neighbor or friend. Yet history tells us that's not the case. Some of the women victims of the Bosnian War, for example, reported being raped by young men who had grown up as playmates with their own children. In Rwanda, Tutsis and Hutus lived side by side. Yet there was an official call to exterminate anyone of Tutsi descent. They were made inhuman in the aggressors' minds. They became dispensable "cockroaches" rather than human persons with individual identities.[1] The pictures of the blood-stained rivers filled with dead, swollen bodies spoke loudly to that terrifying sentiment. Unfortunately, history books and tales from the beginning of time repeat the same tragic scenarios—friends turning against friends, neighbor against neighbor, and even family member against family member. We continue, still, to ask ourselves who these people are who allow such things. Who are these criminals inflicting these terrors and atrocities? The answer is startling.

We are these people. We are all capable of the malady of which we so easily accuse others. We are capable of violence and offense, at an individual and collective level; but in contrast, we also are all immensely capable of love in a broader sense than we normally experience. In May 2003, during a prayer event just before Lent, Pope John Paul II called out this interior human struggle by stating, "In the inner heart of every person, the voice of God and the insidious voice of the Evil One can be heard."[2] He went on to say that one can genuinely overcome this struggle only by praying and following God's will. That is because we are each challenged on a daily basis to choose good over evil. But in order to change, we must act. It starts and ends with us as individuals. At my daughters' school, there is a series of questions stenciled at its entryway. It reads with such simplicity: *"If not us, who? If not here, where? If not now, when?"*

Overall, a spiritual awakening and a changing of heart is accomplished through the regular things we do every day—some known to others; some kept in the silence of our hearts. We don't have to be in the midst of a war or confronted by an extreme situation to demonstrate how to love others deeply and sincerely. Not everyone is called to lead people—as was Martin Luther King Jr., Gandhi, or Pope John Paul II—but we are all called to change the world, according to our own places in life, whether a parent, teacher, volunteer, sister, brother, or shop owner. We are called to make every moment and every interaction filled with love. This means constant vigilance and mastery over our thoughts, behaviors, and actions. It means constantly aspiring to be spiritual and deliberately making the choice for good over evil, in small and large matters. In Luke 16:10,

Jesus explains the parable of the dishonest steward and says, "The person who is trustworthy in very small matters is also trustworthy in great ones; and the person who is dishonest in very small matters is also dishonest in great ones."[3]

I try to practice my spirituality every day by doing common things, like telling the truth, being honest, and speaking up in situations where others may not be willing to speak up. I focus on being respectful of others and using my positions of formal and informal influence to do good for others, rather than exclusively focusing on what is good for me. I strive to be a person of integrity and principle in all that I do, giving credit where credit is due, building people up and looking out for the underdog or the person who cannot help himself or herself, maybe materially or maybe just spiritually. I try to say kind words or share difficult messages in a respectful way. I constantly strive to forgive and ask Jesus to forgive me for those I have hurt or offended. It is not always easy to live according to these basic principles. I have my own faults and weaknesses—everyone does. We are all imperfect by nature, but to genuinely try to improve upon our current situations by changing our outlook and actions is a call for each and every one of us. Sometimes the most common situations in work or family matters allow us to practice this deeper level of spirituality.

A senior professional at work once made false, disparaging comments to others about me that were likely to damage my professional reputation. This person was in a position of authority over me and had the power to affect my employment. I became incensed and thought of confronting him, but it probably would have resulted in negative consequences. I did speak to a colleague about the situation and determined that the best course was to focus on being professional and influencing his perceptions of me going forward. This was very difficult to do but I knew I had to handle the situation constructively. I also knew on a spiritual level that this was an opportunity to approach things differently. I prayed and asked, *What can I do, God? You always say that we are to love our enemies and love those who offend us, but I have no feeling of love for this person, only anger.* I ruminated on this a lot and went back and forth on what my husband calls the slippery slope of anger, where I allow myself to be consumed by bitter thoughts and negativity. Then, through deep reflection, God reminded me of something— hate the sin, not the sinner. People do not equal their actions and I should not vilify this person for his one misstep. After all, I can't just think and write about being spiritual; I have to actually *be* spiritual. But God took it one step further and encouraged me, through inspiration, to do something that I had no desire to do—pray for this person. It felt awkward and insincere, so I asked God for specific guidance on how to pray, and He showed me a path forward. Although I could not, in good conscience, pray for happiness for this person at that moment, I realized that I could pray sincerely for what God wanted for him. Of course, I could not possibly know what God would want for anyone, so I offered the following simple prayer: "Lord Jesus, I pray in my heart for whatever you desire for this person, spiritually—not what I want, Lord, but what you want for this person. Amen." When I offered this prayer, I felt relieved. I wasn't being phony. I still didn't have positive feelings toward this person, but I knew I could not let my feelings consume me.

Saint Faustina wrote in her diary that she did not always particularly feel love toward some people in her life, and this bothered her. Jesus said in a vision to her, "It is not always within your power to control your feelings. You will recognize that you have love if, after having experienced annoyance and contradiction, you don't lose your peace but pray for those who have made you suffer and wish them well."[4] This quote brings me hope and strength, because often I don't feel emotionally good inside about people or situations. But I know if I pray for them, I am following God's will. Of course, I ultimately do hope to be able to feel emotionally better about all my interactions, but I am realistic that it will not always be the case. We are complex human beings with myriad experiences. We will never be fully able to understand one another. I understand now that building each other up is much more fruitful than ripping each other apart. This is what we are up against within ourselves—choosing the right spiritual behavior, fighting the battles of our heart. Gandhi once articulated this concept poignantly when he stated, "The only devils in this world are those running around inside your own hearts, and that is where all our battles should be fought."[5]

Most of us have been told over and over throughout our lives that there are simple gestures we can do to brighten someone's day—a kind look or a smile, for example. It seems so basic and almost trite, but there is something powerful about the simplicity of it. Acts of love are sometimes great but often are small yet very meaningful. They can seem unglamorous and even tedious. I used to regularly visit a great-aunt and developed a very close relationship with her. She was a widow and had lost her only son to cancer. When we started to spend time together, she was in her eighties and lived alone. Many of the basic housekeeping and maintenance issues had become a challenge for her; one, in particular, was grocery shopping. During my visits to her home, I often would go to the store for her, and she was always very appreciative of my help. By and large, I do my own grocery shopping out of necessity, but I do not enjoy it. Isn't it ironic that God put me in a situation where the very thing I didn't like to do was the very thing I could do to help someone else out? I still laugh out loud when I think about it and thank God for my opportunity to serve my aunt in this unique way! Serving her in all aspects was truly a joy for me. Our bond grew so strong that Steve and I named our first daughter, Madeline, after her.

Eventually, my aunt moved to Maine to live in an assisted living community, near my father and his brothers. One day I received a call that she had broken her hip and had been moved to a nursing facility. She had been refusing to eat for almost two weeks and was non-responsive. Steve, Maddy, and I immediately went to Maine to see her. When we walked into the room, I could tell she was uncomfortable—moaning and aching, crying out that she was hot, and kicking off the sheets. I touched her hand and said, "Aunt Madeline, it's me, Amy." To my surprise, she immediately opened her eyes wide and said, "Oh, hello, dear." She squeezed my hand, asking, "Where is the baby?"

"Right here," I said, and Steve brought Maddy over to her side. I told her I was concerned that she wasn't eating and encouraged her to eat. She didn't respond to my comment. We all believed that she had made her decision that she was ready to leave this world. "I love you," I said as I looked at her with sad but accepting resolve.

"I love you, too," she said.

My father, who was in the room with us, said that was the most responsive she had been in two weeks; he was stunned by how attentive to us she was. That was our final visit with my Aunt Madeline. She passed within days of our visit. We believe she was waiting for us to say goodbye. In the years of assisting her, I learned many things, but one great lesson stands out: the small things we do for each other really make a difference.

Over the years I've had many concerns about my ability to write this book and spread the messages of God. I mainly struggled because at different times, I have practiced Mary's messages of peace, faith, fasting, prayer, and conversion with varying levels of zeal and commitment. I thought that if I was not fasting on bread and water every Wednesday and Friday, or if I did not pray the rosary each day, then I was not being an effective witness. But I know that God picks imperfect people to do his work. The following excerpt from Saint Faustina's diary sums it up best. She reports how a priest addressed her concern and worry about doing God's will effectively. From the Diary of Saint Faustina, message #464:

> During a meditation on humility, an old doubt returned: that a soul as miserable as mine could not carry out the task which the Lord was demanding of me. Just as I was analyzing this doubt, the priest who was conducting the retreat interrupted his train of thought and spoke about the very thing I

was having doubts about; namely, that *God usually chooses the weakest and simplest souls as tools for his greatest works . . . for it is just in this way that God's works are revealed for what they are: the works of God.*[6]

If we just open ourselves up to hearing the messages of Medjugorje, hearing the messages of the Gospel and ultimately of Jesus, He will help us do his work.

Twenty-Five

Mary's Season

Every living thing experiences a cycle of growth: a seed is planted, it takes root, it begins to grow, and in the springtime sunlight, it blossoms and reaches maturity. Mary's messages in Medjugorje are very similar. She helps us see the cycle of growth of our souls in the same way that other living organisms grow and thrive. In Medjugorje, the messages are the seeds planted in our hearts. She is asking us to let them take root so that they will help change our hearts to make the world a better place.

During an outing to a museum one day with my daughters, we explored an energy exhibit. It showed how the vibrations from one's voice could trigger a light to turn on. Once the light came on, a small metal flower slowly arched toward the light. On the display was a note about this special phenomenon that read: "Flowers bend toward the light." This simple reality of the flower mirrors the truth of our souls. They bend toward the light of God as He calls us closer to Him. Mary beckons us. In her January 31, 1985, message, she said, "Dear children! Today I wish to tell you to open your hearts to God like the spring flowers, which crave the sun."[1]

It is well known that Mary's signature flower is the rose; it is linked to her throughout history. Mary is seen in paintings and statues surrounded by roses. In Guadalupe, Mexico, Mary left roses as part of a permanent imprint on the cloak of a widower named Juan Diego. Tradition says that Mary appeared in the 1500s to Diego on a hill outside of present-day Mexico City, asking for a shrine to be built in her honor. In order to help him prove to the local bishop that she really was asking for this shrine, Mary filled his coat with fresh roses. When Diego returned to the bishop and the roses fell out, the image of Mary, known as Our Lady of Guadalupe, remained emblazoned on his mantle.[2] Physical and spiritual healings also often are accompanied by the strong fragrance of roses, which is said to signal Mary's presence or healing powers. The rosary prayer was established in the 1500s as a devotion to Mary, and she even has been given the name the "Mystical Rose." In the nineteenth century, the well-known Cardinal Newman of England, a convert to Catholicism, once said, "Mary is the most beautiful flower ever seen in the spiritual world. . . . She is the queen of spiritual flowers and therefore is called the Rose."[3]

This is the season for Mary to cultivate our souls. Mary tells us repeatedly in her messages at Medjugorje that hers is an urgent call and that the time for us to convert our hearts is now. A rose begins as a bud, opens up, and awakens to its season; similarly, this is the season for our souls to awaken. Mary watches over us, caring for us and helping us along our journey. Her messages and instruction help our souls to flourish. In one of her messages she said, "Little children, I wish you to be a beautiful bouquet of flowers which I wish to present to God."[4] As we live the messages of peace, prayer, faith, fasting, and conversion, we will grow spiritually, and our souls will blossom like flowers in the springtime.

Over the years and through hundreds of Mary's messages, questions have been asked about religion and how God perceives us here on earth. Is there one religion? Are we all really children of God? During one of the visionary's apparitions in January 1985, it was recorded that Mary addressed this very question in response to a priest who had become aware of the healing of a gypsy child. He was distressed, not over the healing itself, but the fact that the child was of a different faith and a member of an ethnic group that had viciously persecuted people in the region. Part of Mary's response reminds us of the omnipotent love of God: "Tell this priest, tell everyone, that it is you who are divided on earth. . . . You are all my children. Certainly, all religions are not equal, but all men are equal before God, as Saint Paul says." She went on, "Salvation is available to everyone, without exception. Only those who refuse God deliberately are condemned." And lastly, she reminded us "It is God alone, in His infinite justice who determines the degree of responsibility and pronounces judgment."[5]

Many people ask me if my messages are only about accepting Jesus or if I am telling people to convert to Catholicism. I can only tell you that I believe wholeheartedly in

Jesus as our Savior, and I am a practicing Catholic. I can tell you that going to Medjugorje changed my life for the better and that I hope others will learn more about Medjugorje, so that Mary's universal messages may change individual hearts of all religious persuasions. I am not an expert on Medjugorje, nor am I an expert on world religion, Catholicism, Christianity, or spirituality. I am not in a position to decide for others what they should do, and I do not judge the individual situations that people are in. I am simply a person who saw the hand reach out in a miraculous and divine way and took it. I am now offering to others what I have learned about one of the greatest spiritual events of our time. Throughout the church's history, Mary has made herself visible to the world, to share warnings and to plead with her children to follow God's ways—apparitions have been reported from Japan to Ireland to Mexico. Mary has appeared at various critical times to call people back to God, but these visits from Mary at Medjugorje are the longest standing of any of her visits anywhere. She herself said, ". . . I wish to keep on giving you messages as it has never been in history from the beginning of the world."[6]

The messages of Medjugorje come at a time in history when we face much turmoil and instability. In the past twelve years, the world has witnessed monumental events—the terrorist attacks on the United States, wars in the Middle East, the tsunami in Asia, hurricanes Katrina and Rita in the United States, the earthquake in Japan, genocide in Africa, and the near collapse of the American and global financial system. We are, indeed, in a time of cataclysmic change, and many people are still searching for deeper meanings in their lives.

Many people ask why the Catholic Church has not officially endorsed Medjugorje. It is because the apparitions still occur, and the church reserves final judgment on apparitions until they end. In June 2010, however, the Vatican formed a commission to investigate the apparitions of Mary in Medjugorje.[7] That work is still underway, but as with other private revelations, the church permits the faithful to visit sites and show reverence as long as it does not conflict with the essence of the church's teachings and if it helps followers in their faith. Over the past thirty years, the number of pilgrims visiting Medjugorje is reported to have reached over 30 million.[8]

Although Pope John Paul II never visited Medjugorje, he was noted for giving his blessing to many different people who devoted their lives to its cause. An anecdotal story relates that he said he went to Medjugorje as a pilgrim every day in his prayers. If we could all do that pilgrimage in our hearts, we would truly have peace on earth.

Conclusion

The Journey Continues

A journey is defined as "a trip or expedition from one place to another."[1] In my case, I know from where I am starting but I never quite know to which place I am going. The essence of faith, however, and perhaps the greatest test of faith, is to stay the course, regardless of clarity. Mother Angelica, a nun who founded the largest religious media network in the world, Eternal World Television Network, has defined faith as "one foot on the ground, one foot in the air, and a queasy feeling in your stomach."[2] That just about sums it up for me.

In December 2009, I attended Mass at a nearby church. It was the second Sunday in Advent, leading up to the celebration of Christmas. I participated fully in the Mass, reflecting upon the readings and spending quiet time in prayer after receiving the Holy Eucharist. I attended

Mass alone on this morning, so I was able to focus more on prayer. In fact, I decided to remain in the church after Mass to say a rosary. I knelt down in the pew and began my prayer. I had progressed through four of the five decades of the rosary when my mind turned to the story of Mary's appearances in Fatima, Portugal and the messages of Medjugorje, and how during the past week I had received a very special sign from a friend—and these were all related. For more than five years I have received a daily e-mail that contains either an excerpt from the diary of Saint Faustina or a message detailed in the writings of a woman named Gabrielle Bossis, a French woman who reportedly conversed with Jesus about her daily life and trials. I was taken aback when I opened the message that week and read the following statement that Gabrielle recorded during an exchange. It appealed to me in an uncanny way:

> Write! I don't want people to be afraid of me anymore, but to see my heart full of love and to speak with me as they would with a dearly beloved brother. For some, I am unknown. For others, a stranger, a severe master, or an accuser. And yet my love is there, waiting for them. So tell them to come, to enter in, to give themselves up to love just as they are. Just as they are. I'll restore. I'll transform them. And they will know a joy they have never known before. I alone can give that joy. If only they would come! Tell them to come.[3]

During my prayerful reflection, I was reminded again that Jesus was urging me to write my story. I could not shake the fact that I had received this message and it was as if it was also speaking directly to me. I also thought to myself that I was finally ready. In fact, I wasn't only ready but eager to move on to the next phase of my spiritual life, yet I did not know how it was going to happen. Just as I was about to enter into the final decade of the rosary, I was interrupted by a soft voice that said, "Excuse me." I opened my eyes, emerging from a deep, meditative state of prayer. I looked up and to my right was a woman, standing with her hand outstretched. Without thinking and or hesitation, I took her hand securely, squeezed it, and rose to embrace her. We held hands and hugged for maybe five seconds. Five seconds is a long time to hug a stranger. Yet we understood something about each other without exchanging any initial words. When she did try to speak to me, I quickly learned that she had a limited command of English. She was a short woman, maybe in her fifties, with dark hair and tan-colored skin. She seemed to be of South American descent, perhaps Peruvian. She was gesturing and trying to communicate something to me. I thought I heard her describe Mary, so I asked, "Mary? Mother Mary?" She nodded her head and said, "Yes, Mary." As I looked at her inquisitively, she continued to nod her head and pointed again to the ceiling, and then to me, and back to the ceiling again and said, "Mother Mary blazing."

My eyes widened, as I looked at her doubtfully and asked, "Blazing on me?" I placed my hand over my heart and looked at her in disbelief. "Yes," she said confidently. Although our verbal exchange was limited, she conveyed the information that there was either a literal or figurative light from Mary blazing down upon me as I prayed. I was not sure how to react; in fact, I was stunned. All I could say was "Thank you." She smiled warmly and once again hugged me. She then handed me a 2010 religious calendar, turned from the pew, and disappeared through the back area of the church. Immediately, I made the connection to the description of Mary that Cassidy had made a couple of years back in her hospital room. I was certain that Mary was reaching out to me—Mary, the blazing "warrior for her children." I burst into tears, completely overwhelmed by gratitude for the immense love and support directly provided to me by Jesus and Mary.

Steve and I had long contemplated how the book should conclude and when to publish it, but we were never really clear on the timing. After my encounter with the woman in the church, there was absolute clarity that the book would come to closure soon. As it turned out, the final chapter of the book was written in January 2010, after the following December events:

On Christmas Day, Steve attended Mass at the church in which we were married. He stood alongside my father, thinking of how special it was that my parents had also been married there and had marked their fiftieth wedding anniversary together the previous April. The church was filled with all the prestige and architectural grandeur associated with its status as a minor basilica, and the Christmas décor added to its splendor. Steve had only visited the church on three previous occasions. This day was special for him, not only because it was Christmas, but because he was unusually free to focus on the celebration of the Mass. The children had stayed home with me, as I had attended

Christmas Eve Mass the previous evening with other family members. He was captivated by the experience of the Mass and the spiritual atmosphere permeating the setting on this day. He was startled out of a state of reflection when a man approached him with the offering basket. Steve fumbled to retrieve money from one of the zippered pockets in his jacket, which he'd placed on the seat next to him. The gentleman courteously waited as he pulled out a handful of dollars. A quick count revealed that he only had three one-dollar bills. He knew that he had more money inside the other pocket, and he felt very uncomfortable depositing what felt like an insufficient contribution, especially on Christmas Day. But he placed the three dollars into the basket so that he would no longer hold up the collection process.

As the man withdrew the basket, Steve began to justify in his mind that the three dollars was enough. He knew that I also had made a contribution the night before at the Christmas Eve celebration. His mind started to replay our recent conversations regarding financial planning in the New Year. We had discussed sticking to a tight budget in order to offset some significant spending in 2009. As soon as that thought crossed his mind, another presented itself—this was Christmas Day, the day to celebrate the birth of Jesus and all that He has given us. Certainly, Steve realized, he could spare another twenty dollars to show his faith to Jesus. Steve grabbed a twenty-dollar bill from his other jacket pocket and walked to the back of the church to deposit it into the collection basket. But just as he arrived, the men who collected the offerings had already started carrying them up the center aisle to the altar. Steve had missed his opportunity and was visibly disappointed. He resolved to deposit the twenty-dollar bill into the following Sunday collection. The money had taken on a whole new meaning to him at this point. Now, it symbolized faithful, spiritual giving, rather than his giving only what he felt was sufficient. This sentiment became very relevant for him regarding the book and its publication. At that moment, Steve vowed to not let our New Year's household budget get in the way of our publishing timeline. He knew that 2010 was the year that we must faithfully commit ourselves to this spiritual pursuit and that we must not withhold what God had given us in terms of material gifts. Our gifts should be pointed to doing God's work and spreading the messages of Medjugorje. As that spiritual reflection materialized, Steve happened to glance at the half-folded bill in his hand and noticed there was something written on the bill in red ink. He looked closer and was astonished to read the following inscription: *Jesus Loves You.*

Steve's Christmas message genuinely sums up the essence of this story: God loves each and every one of us and is calling for us to return fully to Him. And Mary, our spiritual mother, is here to guide us along. In a message given December 1984, Mary said, "I want you to be a flower which will blossom for Jesus on Christmas. And a flower that will not stop blooming when Christmas is over. I want your hearts to be shepherds to Jesus."[4]

This Christmas gift will forever be a part of our spiritual journey, not only because it became the final chapter of this story, but also because it was the last Christmas Mass my father attended before he passed into eternal life on April 27, 2010. During his long and tiring dialysis treatments, my father read the entire draft of this story and offered final

pieces of advice to his daughter, whose writing interests he always fervently supported. Most important, however, he helped bring home the conclusion by being a part of that very special Christmas-giving story.

As for Steve and me and the first leg of our spiritual journey, it brings us full circle. In my very first dream, I saw a faceless woman with a wedding ring and received an unintelligible message that had to do with the end of December. Here we were, in the very church where we were married, living out the last chapter in our ten-year spiritual awakening. Although we are not exactly sure what the end of December ultimately signifies, we received direction on how to move forward with the closure of the book. It was finally clear. Maybe in time, the mystery of 7:24 will also reveal itself to us. Or maybe it is as simple as Steve's interpretation: we are called to be spiritual 7 days a week, 24 hours a day, in each and every moment.

Notes

Introduction Transition Page
Mary's Message April 25, 2008

1. Quote from Mary comes from the Information Centre "Mir" Medjugorje website at http://www.medjugorje.hr/ noted as the only official voice of the apparitions in Medjugorje.

Transition Page (chapters 1–3)
Mary's Message January 25, 2008

1. Quote from Mary comes from http://www.medjugorje.com/

Transition Page (chapters 4–6)
Mary's Message September 8, 2006

1. Quote from Mary comes from http://www.medjugorje.com/

Transition Page (chapters 7–10)
Mary's Message April 10, 1986

1. Quote from Mary comes from the Information Centre "Mir" Medjugorje website at http://www.medjugorje.hr/

Chapter 7

1. Weible, Wayne. *Medjugorje, The Message*. Brewster, MA: Paraclete Press, 1989. Written permission from the author was obtained to use and reference material from the book *Medjugorje, The Message*.
2. *Medjugorje* Information Centre "Mir" Medjugorje, 2002.
3. *Medjugorje* Information Centre "Mir" Medjugorje, 2002.
4. *Medjugorje* Information Centre "Mir" Medjugorje, 2002.
5. Information Centre "Mir" Medjugorje website at http://www.medjugorje.hr/
6. *Medjugorje* Information Centre "Mir" Medjugorje, 2002.

Chapter 9

1. Kowalska, Saint Maria Faustina. *Diary, Divine Mercy in My Soul*. Congregation of Marians. First published 1987. Third edition with revisions (13th printing), 2001.

Chapter 11

1. *Medjugorje* Information Centre "Mir" Medjugorje, 2002.

Transition Page (chapters 11–14)
Mary's Message December 18, 1986

1. Quote from Mary comes from the Information Centre "Mir" Medjugorje website at http://www. medjugorje.hr/

Chapter 12

1. *Medjugorje* Information Centre "Mir" Medjugorje, 2002.
2. Information Centre "Mir" Medjugorje website at http://www.medjugorje.hr/
3. Kowalska, Saint Maria Faustina. *Diary, Divine Mercy in My Soul*. Congregation of Marians. First published: 1987. Third edition with revisions (13th printing), 2001.
4. Quote from Mary comes from her message March 28, 1985 on the website http://www.medjugorje.ws/
5. Information Centre "Mir" Medjugorje website at http://www.medjugorje.hr/
6. Saint Joseph Addition of The New American Bible. New York: Catholic Book Publishing Co., 1970.
7. Information Centre "Mir" Medjugorje website at http://www.medjugorje.hr/
8. Excerpts taken from a letter dated December 2, 1983 from Father Tomislav Vlasic to Pope John Paul II, published 9/20/06 under the News & Articles tab on the website http:// www.medjugorje.ws/
9. Weible, Wayne. *Medjugorje, The Message*. Brewster, MA: Paraclete Press, 1989.

Chapter 13
1. Saint Joseph Addition of The New American Bible. New York: Catholic Book Publishing Co., 1970.

Transition Page (chapters 15–20)
Mary's Message January 25, 2010
1. Quote from Mary comes from the Information Centre "Mir" Medjugorje website at http://www.medjugorje.hr/

Chapter 17
1. Twister® is a game by made by the company Hasbro.

Chapter 18
1. *Sun Journal,* Lewiston, Maine 1997 article. Retrieved through Auburn Public Library archives.
2. Information on Rwandan Genocide sited from several sources including *Left to Tell,* BBC News story "Rwanda: How the genocide happened," and Wikipedia.

Chapter 19
1. http://www.internationalcruisevictims.org/

Chapter 20
1. http://catholicism.about.com/
2. St. Jude Novena, as found on copies left in church

Transition Page (chapters 21–25)
Mary's Message February 25, 2010
1. Quote from Mary comes from the Information Centre "Mir" Medjugorje website at http://www.medjugorje.hr/

Chapter 21
1. Saint Joseph Addition of The New American Bible. New York: Catholic Book Publishing Co., 1970.

Chapter 24
1. Information on Rwandan Genocide sited from several sources including *Left to Tell*, BBC News story "Rwanda: How the genocide happened," and Wikipedia.
2. Vatican Archives: Angelus March 9, 2003.
3. Saint Joseph Addition of The New American Bible. New York: Catholic Book Publishing Co., 1970.
4. Kowalska, Saint Maria Faustina. *Diary, Divine Mercy in My Soul*. Congregation of Marians. First published 1987. Third edition with revisions (13th printing), 2001.
5. Mahatma Gandhi quotes online at http://www.spiritual-experiences.com/

6. Kowalska, Saint Maria Faustina. *Diary, Divine Mercy in My Soul.* Congregation of Marians. First published 1987. Third edition with revisions (13th printing), 2001.

Chapter 25
1. Information Centre "Mir" Medjugorje
2. http://www.sancta.org
3. Essay on "The Mystical Rose" at http://home.earthlink.net/~mysticalrose/mystrose.html
4. Information Centre "Mir" Medjugorje website at http://www.medjugorje.hr/
5. Weible, Wayne. *The Final Harvest.* Brewster, MA: Paraclete Press, 1999.
6. Information Centre "Mir" Medjugorje website at http://www.medjugorje.hr/
7. *Vatican Insider*: http://www.vaticaninsider.com/. "Pope to make pronouncement on Medjugorje by 2012." February 25, 2012.
8. *Reuters Life!* http://www.reuters.co.uk/. "Vatican probes claims of apparitions at Medjugorje." March 17, 2010.

Conclusion
1. *Encarta Dictionary*: http://www.memidex.com/journey
2. Arroyo, Raymond. *Mother Angelica's Little Book of Life Lessons and Everyday Spirituality.* New York: Doubleday, 2007.

3. Bossis, Gabrielle. *He and I.* Sherbrooke, QE: Editions Mediaspaul, 1985
4. Information Centre "Mir" Medjugorje website at http://www.medjugorje.hr/

About the Author

Amy Boucher has worked professionally in corporate human resources for Fortune 100 companies for the past fifteen years. She has a bachelor's degree from Clark University and a master's degree from Teachers College, Columbia University. Amy's passion for writing developed at an early age, and as a high school student, she wrote for the *Sun Journal*, a local Maine newspaper. In 1987 she was awarded a scholarship from the Maine Media Woman's Association in support of her writing pursuits. In addition to writing, Amy enjoys reading religious and spiritual books, running, skiing, and spending time with her family. She lives with her husband and two daughters in Connecticut.

CPSIA information can be obtained at www.ICGtesting.com
Printed in the USA
BVOW08s1609290813

329659BV00005B/10/P